ESTIMATING VALUE-ADDED TAX USING A SUPPLY AND USE FRAMEWORK

THE ADB NATIONAL ACCOUNTS STATISTICS VALUE-ADDED TAX MODEL

FEBRUARY 2024

ASIAN DEVELOPMENT BANK

Notes:
In this publication, "$" refers to United States dollars.
ADB recognizes "China" as the People's Republic of China and "Republic of Armenia" as Armenia.

Cover design by Eric Suan.

On the cover: (1 and 5) Market scene at the Gum Market in Yerevan, Armenia (photo by Eric Sales). (2) A man is selling dried fruits and delicacies at the green market in Almaty City, Kazakhstan (photo by Andrey Terekhov). (3) Daily life in Samarkand market, Uzbekistan (photo by Relisa Granovskaya); (4) Improved health services in Artashat, Armenia (photo by Inna Mkhitaryan). (6 and 7) Hamkorbank branch in Samarkand, Uzbekistan, providing sub loans to small businesses in the project with ADB (photo by Relisa Granovskaya).(8) ADB administration and governance, finance sector development (photo by Mark Floro). (9) School boy receiving water in the town of Artashat, Armenia for improved cleanliness and health of the students (photo by Inna Mkhitaryan).

Printed on recycled paper

CONTENTS

TABLES, FIGURES, AND BOXES

FOREWORD

Value-added taxes (VATs) have been adopted by many countries as an effective, stable and broad-based means of generating significant revenues for the government. Moreover, the VAT's mechanism of cascading taxes is appealing from the point of view of production efficiency as it creates less distortion in production and input choices. Under this mechanism, producers can deduct the VAT they pay on their purchases against the VAT they charge on their sales.

Given their broad coverage, VAT measurements are useful indicators for economic and fiscal analyses and play a crucial role in validating gross domestic product estimates and ensuring consistency of the national accounts estimates through the supply and use framework. This publication proposes an estimation model, the Asian Development Bank (ADB) National Accounts Statistics VAT Model Using the Supply and Use Framework (NAS-VAT model), which provides a more theoretically consistent measure of VAT and its impact on the producing sectors through the VAT gap and the theoretical VAT ratio of an economy. The model can be used to refine and balance the supply and use tables. Moreover, the ADB NAS-VAT model can be used not only to assess the strength of the VAT administration and the consistency of national accounts estimates, but also to simulate alternate tax regimes and scenarios. This publication also presents analyses which apply the model to select developing member countries.

The knowledge support and technical assistance—under the regional projects on (i) Data for Development (Phase 2) (TA 9646-REG), and (ii) Supporting Knowledge Solutions in Central and West Asian Countries (Phase 2) (TA 6958-REG)—provided tailored support to national statistical offices in ADB's Central and West Asia Region. One output of these regional technical assistance projects are the VAT matrices for Armenia, Kazakhstan, and Uzbekistan, which extensively use the ADB NAS-VAT model. The tax matrices provide especially useful data frameworks for assessing the tax reform measures being studied by relevant national agencies in collaboration with the International Monetary Fund.

This technical publication was prepared by experts in the field of macroeconomic accounting, led by Mahinthan Joseph Mariasingham and under the overall direction of Elaine S. Tan. The core research team included Gienneen G. Antonio, Jahm Mae E. Guinto, and Dean Joseph A. Villanueva. The model, sources, methods, and results were presented to and discussed with officials from national statistical offices at an ADB–Islamic Development Bank regional conference. This publication also benefited from the significant contributions of Julieta Magallanes and Ana Francesca Rosales for their meaningful insights on the intricacies of the supply and use framework; Anna Monina Sanchez for the supply and use tables coordination work for Armenia; Sarah Mae Manuel for the same for Kazakhstan and Uzbekistan; Dale Maverenz Lim and Maegan Saroca for their work on the gross fixed capital formation matrices for the different countries; and Angelo Jose Lumba and Eric Suan for excellent technical and administrative support. This publication also received feedback from Eric Hutton, Stefano Pisani, and Shan Zhong from the International Monetary Fund Fiscal Affairs Department. The cover of this publication was designed by the VAT team. Terry E. Clayton edited the manuscript, while Joe Mark Ganaban led the layout, page design, and typesetting process.

We hope that this publication can help macroeconomic accounts compilers, official statisticians, government officials, researchers, and development practitioners in Asia and the Pacific gain a deeper understanding and appreciation of the measurement and assessment of VAT and the compilation of national accounts statistics. We also hope that this publication will not only help guide the analysis of fiscal efficiency through the measurement and assessment of VAT, but will also assist statisticians, analysts, and national accountants in the consistent estimation of VATs.

Albert F. Park
Chief Economist and Director General
Economic Research and Development Impact Department
Asian Development Bank

ABBREVIATIONS

DMC	developing member country
GVA	gross value-added
HMRC	HM Revenue and Customs
IMF	International Monetary Fund
NAS-VAT	National Accounts Statistics Value-Added Tax
NOE	Non-observed economy
NPI	Nonprofit institutions
OECD	Organisation for Economic Co-operation and Development
SUT	Supply and use tables
TLS	Taxes less subsidies on products
TTM	Trade and transport margins
TVR	Theoretical VAT ratio
VAT	Value-Added Taxes
VG	VAT gap
VTTL	VAT Total Theoretical Liability

EXECUTIVE SUMMARY

In this publication, the authors propose an estimation model for nonrecoverable Value-Added Taxes (VATs) on products for national accounts statistics. The Asian Development Bank National Accounts Statistics Value-Added Tax (NAS-VAT) model has three major contributions to existing literature on national accounts statistics compilation. First, it offers a theoretically consistent measure of nonrecoverable VAT on products. Supply and Use Tables (SUTs) map out the transformations of products as it moves along the stages of production, and therefore can articulate the input-credit mechanism feature of the prevailing tax laws in question.

Second, the NAS-VAT model allows for the estimation of the VAT impact on producing sectors, by calculating the VAT that is absorbed as costs to production of VAT-exempt producers. This allows policymakers to assess the broadness of the VAT base, given that a sound VAT policy is one that is broad-based, to minimize the economic distortion of VAT on the input choices of producing sectors.

Last, the NAS-VAT model can be used iteratively with the construction and the balancing of the related SUT, revealing inconsistencies between product supplies and the corresponding product use at every iteration. As the SUT approximates the supply and use system of the economy (i.e., as the supply and use are balanced), the iterative application of the NAS-VAT model also approximates the nonrecoverable VAT on each product in the economy.

While the demand for detailed and disaggregated data is high for the application of the NAS-VAT model, the methodology is relatively simple and easy to apply once its salient elements (the policy variables, the taxable proportion, and the isolation rate) had already been defined. Its consistency with the supply and use system makes it highly attractive to policymakers who rely on data and evidence to generate meaningful policies.

The supply and use tables (SUTs) are statistical and analytical tools essential for producing reliable national accounts statistics by balancing an economy's supply and demand. Compilation of data for the SUTs entails considerable complexity as information collected by various agencies must be combined to generate one consistent supply and use system. Among the elements of the SUT that are difficult to compile are the nonrecoverable taxes on products.[1] It is crucial to compile these taxes in a theoretically consistent manner because available data are compiled in aggregate and do not match the requirements of the System of National Accounts (SNA) 2008.

Among different taxes, value-added tax (VAT) is the most difficult to compile because of unique characteristics that make estimation less straightforward for national accounts purposes. VAT is calculated under an input-credit mechanism. Under this mechanism, the computation of VAT liability allows producers to deduct the VAT they pay on their purchases (the input VAT) against the VAT they charge on their sales (the output VAT).

This publication proposes an estimation model for nonrecoverable VAT on products for national accounts statistics—the Asian Development Bank National Accounts Statistics Value-Added Tax (NAS-VAT model). The main estimation challenge in using the SUTs is isolating the VAT embedded in the use data, which are stated in buyers' prices (purchaser's prices). A further difficulty is imposed in that not all producers pay the same VAT rate because there are differences in the status of the value-added taxability of the products each producer supplies.

The NAS-VAT model makes three significant contributions to the literature on national accounts statistics compilation. First, it offers a theoretically consistent measure of nonrecoverable VAT on products. SUTs map the transformations of products as they move along the stages of production and, therefore, can articulate the input-credit mechanism feature of the prevailing tax laws. The existing literature focuses only on the computation of theoretical VAT to estimate VAT gaps (Hutton 2017) (HM Revenue and Customs 2022), and while it offers product-level disaggregation, the orientation of the methodology is sector-based. While the model's primary purpose is to supplement national accounts compilation, the model can also be used to assess the VAT gap in the economy.

---

[1] Nonrecoverable taxes are taxes payable by a purchaser of goods and services that are not deductible from his own VAT liability (System of National Accounts 2008), or not recovered as tax credits. It can be any tax imposed by a jurisdiction on economic transactions.

Second, the model allows for an estimation of the VAT impact on producing sectors by calculating the VAT absorbed as costs to the production of VAT-exempt producers. This allows policymakers to assess the breadth of the VAT base, given that a sound VAT policy is broad-based to minimize the economic distortion of VAT on the input choices of producing sectors.

Last, the model can be used iteratively to construct and balance the related SUT, thereby revealing inconsistencies between product supplies and the corresponding product use at every iteration. As the SUT approximates the supply and use system of the economy (i.e., as the supply and use are balanced), the iterative application of the model also approximates the nonrecoverable VAT on each product in the economy.

A secondary but equally important result of the model is a measure of the VAT gap in any jurisdiction for which a supply and use framework is available. Provided there is a consistent and sufficiently accurate SUT, this statistic will be critically relevant in post-crisis economies. Assessing the VAT gap can help improve domestic resource mobilization through more focused VAT collection, especially for those countries with limited fiscal space due to increased government spending on pandemic health care and narrow tax revenues from slow economic growth.

Section 2 discusses the necessary concepts of value-added taxation and the supply and use framework. Following this, this publication details estimation methodologies in the published literature, focusing on the differences between the NAS-VAT model and these other methodologies. The model is explained in detail in Section 4 and includes a definition of the salient elements of the model, namely, the policy variables, the taxable proportion, the nonrecoverable rate, the VAT gap, and the Theoretical VAT Ratio. Section 5 shows how the model is used in conjunction with balancing the SUTs. Section 6 presents the model's results in Armenia, Kazakhstan, and Uzbekistan. Finally, Section 7 concludes by detailing several policy implications and analyses.

2 CONCEPTUAL BACKGROUND

It is imperative to understand two key concepts to fully grasp the NAS-VAT model: VATs and the SUTs. The model acts as a link that ties these two concepts to generate consistent and reliable estimates of product-disaggregated nonrecoverable VAT. The nexus between VAT and the SUTs is shown in Figure 2.1.

Figure 2.1: Nonrecoverable VAT as the Link between VAT Legislation and the Supply and Use Tables

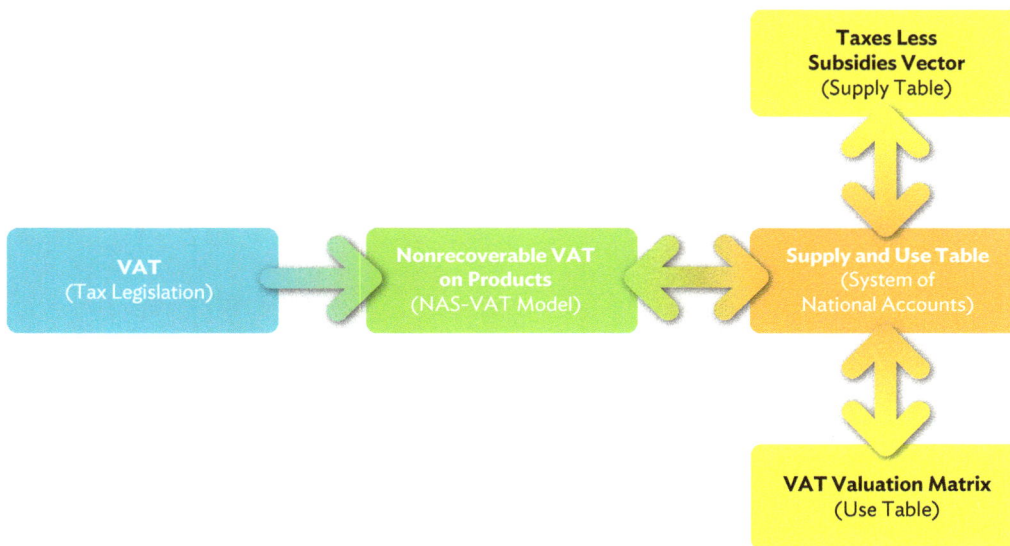

```
                                              ┌──────────────────────┐
                                              │    Taxes Less         │
                                              │   Subsidies Vector    │
                                              │   (Supply Table)      │
                                              └──────────────────────┘
                                                        ⇕
┌─────────────┐      ┌──────────────────┐    ┌──────────────────────┐
│    VAT      │ ──►  │ Nonrecoverable VAT│◄─► │ Supply and Use Table  │
│(Tax         │      │   on Products     │    │   (System of          │
│Legislation) │      │  (NAS-VAT Model)  │    │   National Accounts)  │
└─────────────┘      └──────────────────┘    └──────────────────────┘
                                                        ⇕
                                              ┌──────────────────────┐
                                              │ VAT Valuation Matrix  │
                                              │    (Use Table)        │
                                              └──────────────────────┘
```

NAS-VAT Model = Asian Development Bank National Accounts Statistics Value-Added Tax Model, VAT = value-added tax.
Note: The taxes less subsidies vector is found in the supply table, while the VAT valuation matrix is extracted from the use table.
Source: Authors.

The input-credit mechanism that governs the concept of VAT is generally accepted across jurisdictions. However, the mechanism's features are uniquely governed by each jurisdiction's tax legislation. Meanwhile, the concepts that govern the compilation of the SUTs are provided by the System of National Accounts (SNA). To be reliable for policy purposes, nonrecoverable VAT on products must be consistent with both the tax legislation and the SNA.

2.1. Value-Added Tax

VAT is an indirect consumption tax charged on the sales of goods and services by a taxable person in the ordinary course of business.[2] Its conceptualization can be traced back to the early 1900s as a way to minimize the cascading effects of traditional turnover taxes by introducing an input-credit mechanism (James 2015; Schnek, Thuronyi, and Cui 2015). Unlike traditional turnover taxes, where taxes cascade or become larger the more production stages there are between producer and consumer, the input-credit mechanism allows producers to offset the VAT paid on their own purchases of goods and services (i.e., input VAT) against the tax charged on the related sales (i.e., output VAT) (Schnek, Thuronyi, and Cui 2015; Ebrill et al. 2001). As such, the universal adoption of VAT in any economy will result in producers bearing zero taxes on their inputs. This makes VAT a highly desired consumption tax because it minimizes the economic distortion of input choices (ten Raa 2005).

VAT has significant potential for raising government revenue. Among Organisation for Economic Co-operation and Development (OECD) countries, VAT is the largest source of revenue from taxes on general consumption and a significant source of tax revenue, representing approximately 20.3% of total tax revenue and 6.7% of gross domestic product (GDP) in 2019 (OECD 2020). Among the ADB developing member countries (DMCs) in Figure 2.2, VAT comprises an even larger proportion of total tax revenues at approximately 34% in 2019. As a percentage of GDP, the VAT-to-GDP ratio of select ADB DMCs was 6.1% in 2019. In 2020, amid the public health crisis, VAT remained a major source of tax revenue, comprising approximately 32.5% of total tax collections and 5.4% of GDP during the first year of the pandemic.

As a result of the prominence of VAT, it has seen widespread use since its conception. As of 2020, approximately 170 economies have adopted VAT, with the United States being the only major economy with no federal VAT (Kristoffersson 2021) (OECD 2020).[3]

---

[2] Consumption tax is a tax levied on what people spend on goods and services instead of what they earn (i.e., income tax). It is also called expenditures tax, consumed-income tax, or cashflow tax (Ehrbar n.d.)

[3] While there is no federal VAT, the United States has state consumption taxes.

Figure 2.2: Actual VAT Collections in Select ADB Developing Member Countries 2000–2020

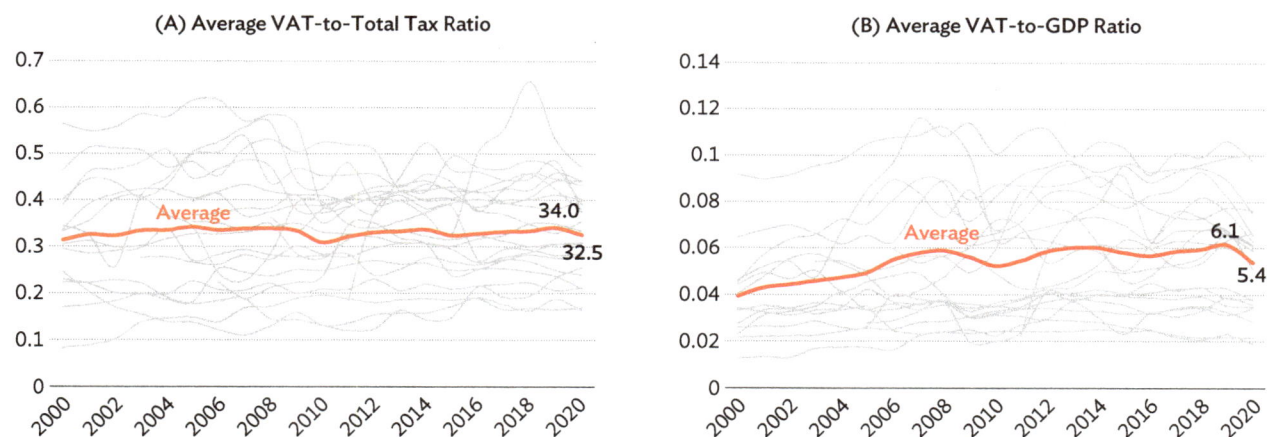

(A) Average VAT-to-Total Tax Ratio

(B) Average VAT-to-GDP Ratio

ADB = Asian Development Bank, GDP = gross domestic product, VAT = value-added tax.
Note: Select ADB developing member countries are Armenia (2000–2020), Azerbaijan (2000–2020), Bangladesh (2000–2020), Cambodia (2005–2020), People's Republic of China (2007–2020), Cook Islands (2006–2020), Fiji (2008–2020), Georgia (2000–2020), Indonesia (2000–2020), Kazakhstan (2020–2020), Kyrgyz Republic (2000–2020), Lao People's Democratic Republic (2010–2020), Malaysia (2015–2018), Maldives (2011–2020), Mongolia (2006–2020), Pakistan (2000–2020), Papua New Guinea (2000–2020), Philippines (2000–2020), Samoa (2005–2020), Singapore (2000–2020), Thailand (2000–2020), Vanuatu (2000–2020), and Viet Nam (2003–2020). The simple average is taken for available years. Appendix 2 shows a summary of ADB developing member country adoption of VAT.
Sources: OECD Stat Revenue Statistics, Asia and the Pacific: Comparative tables, extracted on 16 August 2022. Ministry of Finance of Georgia. Statistical Committee of the Republic of Armenia (through CEIC). The State Statistical Committee of the Republic of Azerbaijan (through CEIC).

Concepts and Definitions

The tax legislation details the country's VAT regime, which is characterized by the VAT rates, its coverage (or base), and other complexities. In an ideal setting, VAT is imposed universally on all goods and services sold in an economy (i.e., broad-based) using the destination principle (James 2015). This implies that producers can perfectly shift the burden of taxation to their customers, and only final consumers (households) pay the VAT.

The destination principle defines the jurisdictional reach of VAT, that is, within the country of consumption (Schnek, Thuronyi, and Cui 2015).[4] Therefore, only goods and services consumed within domestic territories are subjected to a positive rate of VAT, known as the standard rate. Meanwhile, goods and services consumed outside the domestic territory (e.g., exports) are subjected to a zero rate of VAT. Other jurisdictions also have a reduced VAT rate, which is a positive rate lower than the standard VAT rate. Following the inverse elasticity rule, a reduced VAT rate is commonly imposed on commodities for which demand is relatively more elastic, such that a lower VAT rate will have less distortionary impacts on consumption patterns (Ebrill et al. 2001).

---

4   An alternative to the destination principle is the origin principle, which defines the tax jurisdiction to be the country where the goods are produced and services are rendered (Schenk et al. 2015).

Standard, zero, and reduced VAT rates uphold the input-credit mechanism, albeit at differing rates applicable to sales of taxable products. For example, a producer that sells products subject to a zero VAT rate would have an output VAT of zero (i.e., sales × 0%), which is then deductible by the input VAT of the same producer's purchases. Therefore, a producer with zero-rated sales only, say an exclusive exporter of goods, would mostly have VAT refunds from the government.

In some cases, however, output is difficult to tax due to impracticalities, such as further distortion of competition between public and private providers and challenges in identifying taxable outputs. One way to address such concerns is a zero-rating output that is difficult to tax. However, this could be costly for two reasons: (i) zero rating reduces government revenue, and (ii) regulating VAT refunds incur additional administration costs. This led to the development of a middle ground which is VAT exemption. As with a zero VAT rate, output that is VAT-exempt would have a zero output of VAT. In contrast with zero-rating, however, the related input VAT on purchases is not deductible. In effect, VAT exemption breaks the VAT chain along the stages of production.[5]

There is a pattern among economies regarding products that are VAT-exempt. This includes education, health, and financial services. These are commonly rendered as VAT-exempt for education and health to avoid further distorting the competition between the government and private providers.[6] For financial services, these are VAT-exempt because of difficulties in identifying the appropriate tax output, which the market does not explicitly reveal. Moreover, for practical reasons, several small traders with sales falling below a certain threshold are exempted from VAT because administration and compliance costs to include them in the VAT system are not justified by the VAT revenue that accrues from their sales (Ebrill et al. 2001).

Illustrations of Stages of Production

Three scenarios illustrate the input-credit mechanism and the impact of VAT exemption and zero rating at any stage of production: first is when output in all stages of production is subject to the standard rate of VAT, second is when the output of a particular stage is VAT-exempt, and third when the VAT of a given output is zero-rated. Through the VAT input-credit mechanism, producers effectively do not bear the impact of the taxation but only the obligation to collect and remit VAT to the government. Households, final consumers, generally bear the impact of VAT on the goods and services they purchase.

---

[5] If a VAT exemption is imposed on a product at the early stages of production, the non-deductible input VAT cascades through the subsequent stages and potentially undoes, to some extent, the principal merit of VAT (i.e., the non-distortion of input choices of producers) (Ebrill et al. 2001).

[6] Competition is distorted for goods and services sold by both public and private providers as public providers commonly offer prices at below market value. Exempting these types of products promotes parity between private and public providers (Ebrill et al. 2001).

Output of all stages is subject to the standard rate of VAT

Figure 2.3 illustrates how the input-credit mechanism works in stages of production, assuming all products are subject to the standard rate of VAT, which in this example is 10%. When the stage 1 producer sells $100 worth of goods to the stage 2 producer, the latter pays $110 to the former ($100 as the cost of the goods and $10 as the VAT). The stage 1 producer remits the $10 output VAT to the government, the stage 2 producer books the $10 as a creditable input VAT, and only $100 is considered as the cost of inputs.

Figure 2.3: Value-Added Tax Paid in Stages of Production

Goods and services sold in all stages subject to the standard rate of VAT.

Item	Stage 1	Stage 2	Stage 3	Stage 4	Stage 5	FC
Output sold from stage n to stage n+1	100	200	400	500	800	
Less: Cost of inputs of stage n from stage n-1	0	100	200	400	500	800
Value-added	100	100	200	100	300	
Output VAT	10	20	40	50	80	
Less: Input VAT	0	10	20	40	50	80
VAT payable (refund) to the government from stage n	10	10	20	10	30	
Paid on purchases by FC (= purchase by FC from stage 5 + output VAT of stage 5)						880
Tax collected by government (= total VAT payable from stage 1 to 5)						80

FC = final consumer, VAT = value-added tax.
Note: The assumption is that stage 1 only uses primary inputs (labor and capital). The standard rate of VAT is 10%. Output sold from stage n to stage n + 1 is net of VAT. The amount paid on purchases by the final consumer is gross of VAT.
Source: Authors.

In the following stage, when the stage 2 producer sells $200 worth of goods to the stage 3 producer, the latter pays $220 to the former ($200 as the cost of the goods and $20 as the VAT). This time, before the stage 2 producer remits the $20 output VAT to the government, it reduces the amount by the creditable input VAT of $10 from its stage 1 purchases. The stage 2 producer remits a net VAT of $10 ($20 minus $10) to the government. Effectively, the stage 2 producer bore no burden from taxation because the $10 it remitted was collected from stage 3 after offsetting its own input VAT payments to stage 1. Such is the essence of the input-credit mechanism.

Thus far, the government has collected a total of $20 from both stage 1 and stage 2 producers, with each stage remitting $10. From stage 3 to stage 5, the same input-credit mechanism applies. When the product reaches the final consumer, the consumer pays the stage 5 producer a sum comprising the cost ($800) and the VAT ($80) of the product (i.e., a total of $880). Because the final consumer does not sell but only consumes the product, they have no output VAT against which they can offset the VAT paid. In effect, the final consumer bears the impact of the VAT from the entire stage of production. Adding up the VAT payable at each stage, the total VAT remitted to the government is $80 ($10 + $10 + $20 + $10 + $30), which is equal to the VAT paid by the final consumer to the retailer. Therefore, the VAT ultimately borne by the final consumer is remitted in a staggered fashion through all stages of production.

Output of one stage is VAT exempt

If any one product in the stages of production is VAT exempt, the total VAT collected by the government is borne by both the VAT-exempt seller and the final consumer. This is because producers with VAT-exempt sales are not permitted to claim their input VAT for a refund or deduct it against output VAT. Figure 2.4 illustrates this case using stage 2 output VAT-exempt stage. The standard rate of VAT is still 10% in this example.

Figure 2.4: Value-Added Tax Paid in Stages of Production

Sales of stage 2 are VAT-exempt; the rest are subject to a standard rate.

Item	Stage 1	Stage 2	Stage 3	Stage 4	Stage 5	FC
Output sold from stage n to stage n+1	100	210	410	510	810	
Less: Cost of inputs of stage n from stage n-1	0	110	210	410	510	810
Value-added	100	100	200	100	300	
Output VAT	10	0	41	51	81	
Less: Input VAT	0	10	0	41	51	81
VAT payable (refund) to the government from stage n	10	0	41	10	30	
Paid on purchases by FC (= purchase by FC from stage 5 + output VAT of stage 5)						891
Tax collected by government (= total VAT payable from stage 1 to 5)						91

FC = final consumer, VAT = value-added tax.
Note: The assumption is that stage 1 only uses primary inputs (labor and capital). The standard rate of VAT is 10%. Output sold from stage n to stage n+1 is net of VAT. Amount paid on purchases by final consumer is gross of VAT.
Source: Authors.

Only stage 2 output sales are VAT-exempt, not the input purchases. Thus, when the stage 2 producer purchases inputs from stage 1, they still have to pay input VAT of $10. This $10 input VAT is nonrecoverable by the stage 2 producer because their sales to stage 3 producers are VAT-exempt. The stage 2 producer remits nothing to the government and bears the $10 input VAT cost. This becomes embedded in the cost of its inputs ($110). Because stage 2 producers are not precluded from recovering this cost, they raise output prices of their sales to stage 3 producers ($210).

Stage 3 producers purchase VAT-exempt outputs from stage 2 producers; hence, their input VAT is nil. This does not affect the value-added taxability of its own output sales to stage 4 producers. When they make a sale, stage 3 producers act as an intermediary that remits the entire output VAT of $41 to the government. From stage 3 producers onward, the input-credit mechanism applies such that each producer could reduce output VAT on their sales by the input VAT on their purchases. When the product reaches the final consumer, the consumer pays the stage 5 producer a sum comprising the cost ($810) and the VAT ($81) of the product (i.e., $891). The total VAT collected by the government is equal to the sum of the remittances at all stages, which is $91 ($10 + $41 + $10 + $30). It is now apparent that the burden of the $91 VAT is split between the stage 2 producers that absorbed $10 input VAT and the final consumers that bore an $81 VAT on their purchases.

Observe that the total VAT collected in the base case where the output of all stages is subject to VAT ($80, Figure 2.3) is lower than the total VAT collected in the case where stage 2 output is VAT-exempt ($91, Figure 2.4). Holding other factors constant and assuming products sold by VAT-exempt stage 2 producers are perfectly inelastic such that they can pass on the cost of taxation by raising output prices, this phenomenon sheds light on two potential implications of VAT exemption. First, government revenues potentially increase (holding other factors constant) because the government is collecting taxes from final consumers and VAT-exempt producers. Second, the nonrecoverable input VAT of at least one producer (stage 2 in this illustration) introduces distortions on the input choices of other producers because the impact of taxation in an earlier stage cascades through the subsequent stages through the rise in output prices of the VAT-exempt producer.

Output of one stage is zero rated

VAT exemption and zero-rating have one similarity, i.e., the related output VAT of the VAT-exempt product (Figure 2.4) and a zero-rated product (Figure 2.5) are both nil. In terms of the impact of taxation, VAT exemption and zero rating are the opposite. On the one hand, producers selling VAT-exempt output are not allowed to recover their input VAT via the input-credit mechanism, resulting in VAT-exempt producers bearing the burden of taxation on their input purchases. On the other hand, producers selling zero-rated output benefit from the input-credit mechanism as they can claim an input VAT refund from the government. Figure 2.5 illustrates this case, supposing stage 2 output is zero-rated. The standard rate of VAT is still 10% in this example.

In Figure 2.5, when stage 2 producers purchase from stage 1, they still pay input VAT of $10. However, unlike the case when stage 2 producers are VAT-exempt, stage 2 producers selling zero-rated products can claim a refund for the input VAT from the government. In other words, a zero rating does not disrupt the input-credit mechanism. In the final stage, final consumers still bear the total impact of taxation ($80) as in the case when all stages are subject to the standard rate of VAT. However, the amount remitted at each stage is different. Stage 1 producers remit $10, stage 3 $40, stage 4 $10, and stage 5 $30. Stage 2 producers file for an input VAT refund of $10. Hence, the total remittance net of refund is $80.

Figure 2.5: Value-Added Tax Paid in Stages of Production

Sales of stage 2 are zero-rated, and the rest are subject to a standard rate.

Item	Stage 1	Stage 2	Stage 3	Stage 4	Stage 5	FC
Output sold from stage n to stage n+1	100	200	400	500	800	
Less: Cost of inputs of stage n from stage n-1	0	100	200	400	500	800
Value-added	100	100	200	100	300	
Output VAT	10	0	40	50	80	
Less: Input VAT	0	10	0	40	50	80
VAT payable (refund) to the government from stage n	10	(10)	40	10	30	
Paid on purchases by FC (= purchase by FC from stage 5 + output VAT of stage 5)						880
Tax collected by government (= total VAT payable from stage 1 to 5)						80

FC = final consumer, VAT = value-added tax.
Note: The assumption is that stage 1 only uses primary inputs (labor and capital). The standard rate of VAT is 10%. Output sold from stage n to stage n+1 is net of VAT. Amount paid on purchases by the final consumer is gross of VAT.
Source: Authors.

Since the total VAT collected by the government is the same for the case where all stages are subject to the standard rate of VAT (Figure 2.3) and the case where at least one intermediate stage is zero-rated (Figure 2.5), it is implied that the total VAT collected by the government is unaffected if the zero-rated product is purely an intermediate input (i.e., only sold via business-to-business transactions).

If the zero-rated product is purely a final good or service, then zero-rating erases the VAT collectible from all stages of production. Figure 2.6 illustrates this case, where only the products of stage 5 producers are zero-rated. When stage 5 producers sell to a final consumer, the final consumer pays no VAT, and stage 5 producers file to claim a refund of $50. The input VAT refund completely nets out the VAT remitted by stage 1 to stage 4 producers of $50 ($10 + $10 + $20 + $10), leaving a net VAT collection of nil.

Non-registration to the VAT System

Setting registration thresholds simplifies tax matters from the perspective of micro and small enterprises and establishments regarding registration and accounting for VAT.

Setting registration thresholds is based on a trade-off between the taxpayer's compliance costs and the VAT administration's effectiveness. Setting thresholds is contextual. For developing and transitional economies, the recommendation is to set high registration thresholds given the large size of the informal economy and where the compliance capacity of the taxpayer is costly, and the state's administrative capacity is limited (James 2015).

Figure 2.6: Value-Added Tax Paid in Stages of Production

Sales of stage 5 are zero-rated and the rest are subject to a standard rate.

Item		Stage 1	Stage 2	Stage 3	Stage 4	Stage 5	FC
Output sold from stage n to stage n+1		100	200	400	500	800	
Less: Cost of inputs of stage n from stage n-1		0	100	200	400	500	800
Value-added		100	100	200	100	300	
Output VAT		10	20	40	50	0	
Less: Input VAT		0	10	20	40	50	0
VAT payable (refund) to the government from stage n		10	10	20	10	(50)	
Paid on purchases by FC (= purchase by FC from stage 5 + output VAT of stage 5)							800
Tax collected by government (= total VAT payable from stage 1 to 5)							0

FC = final consumer, VAT = value-added tax.
Note: The assumption is that stage 1 only uses primary inputs (labor and capital). The standard rate of VAT is 10%. Output sold from stage n to stage n+1 is net of VAT. Amount paid on purchases by the final consumer is gross of VAT.
Source: Authors.

There are three effects of setting registration thresholds (i) entities do not report taxable sales, (ii) by virtue of the exemption they are denied input tax credits, and (iii) their customers are also denied credit for tax paid on their supplied products (James 2015). These effects are reminiscent of the numerical illustration in the exemption of output in Figure 2.4. Within the stages of production, calculated VAT decreases by the output of non-registered enterprises while it simultaneously increases by its absorption of the VAT imposed on its inputs. On the other hand, VAT decreases the final consumption as the non-registered entities have already absorbed the tax. In this respect, the level of VAT estimated in comparison to the assumption of the absence of the non-registration would vary depending on whether the products being produced by enterprises falling below the registration threshold are an intermediate consumption or a final demand.

VAT systems in many economies, however, allow voluntary registration. The incentives for small businesses to register with the system are the ability to recover VAT on their costs and the preference of businesses along their supply chain to deal only with VAT-registered businesses (Muthitacharoen, Wanichthaworn and Burong 2021).

2.2. The Supply and Use Framework

The supply and use framework provides a neat and systematic way to summarize all economic transactions in an economy. Supply and use tables (SUTs) constitute a key feature of national accounts, as it allows for balancing supply and demand in an economy.

The Supply Table

The supply table (Figure 2.7) shows the supply of goods and services by product and supplying sector, with products appearing as row headers and the supplying sector as column headers (European Commission 2008). To read the supply table in Figure 2.7, for example, for the agriculture sector, the amount of $5,900 is the value of agricultural products it supplies. In the same way, the amount of manufacturing products and services supplied by the agriculture sector is $100 and $150, respectively. In the economy, the agriculture sector supplies products with a total value of $6,150, where agricultural products are considered its primary outputs and manufacturing and services products are its secondary outputs.

The supply table draws a distinction between the output of domestic sectors ($77,220 in Figure 2.7) and imports ($27,570 in Figure 2.7). The production matrix presents the supply of products produced by the domestic sectors. Meanwhile, the vector of imports presents the economy's imports by type of product. For example, the total imports of manufacturing products in the economy (notwithstanding the importing sector) are $20,000.

Data in the production matrix of the supply table is stated in basic prices, which means that it is valued at the amount receivable by the producer from the buyer minus any tax payable (e.g., output VAT) plus any subsidy receivable (United Nations 2010).[7] Basic prices also exclude any transport charges invoiced separately by the producer.

Because the use table is stated in purchaser's prices, the total supply in purchaser's prices is computed for comparability.[8] To determine the total supply in purchaser's prices, the margins, transport charges paid by the purchaser, and nonrecoverable taxes (net of subsidies) are added to each product's total supply at basic prices. Margins and transport charges are contained in the vector for trade and transport margins (TTM), while nonrecoverable taxes (net of subsidies) are included in the vector for taxes less subsidies (TLS) on products.

The TTM vector shows the sum of TTM by product type. Trade margin is "the difference between the actual or imputed price realized on a good purchased for resale and the price that would have to be paid by the distributor to replace the good when it is sold or otherwise disposed of" (United Nations 2010). Meanwhile, transport margins are charges paid separately by the purchaser for the delivery of goods. The TTM vector adds up to nil because only a reallocation of margins from

---

[7] Imports are usually valued at cost, insurance and freight (CIF), which is already comparable to the domestic production of goods at basic prices. Nonetheless, a CIF/Free on Board (FOB) adjustment is made to make the total imports comparable and consistent with the recommendations of the 2008 System of National Accounts and the Balance of Payments.

[8] The purchaser's price is valued at the amount paid by the buyer, that is, including nonrecoverable taxes absorbed, margins, and any transport charges paid by the purchaser (SNA 2008).

the outputs of the wholesale and retail trade sector (for trade margins) and the transportation sector (for transport margins) is made to the respective products where the margins are associated.[9] In (Figure 2.7) this is calculated by subtracting margins amounting to $8,800 from services products (presumably containing the wholesale and retail trade and transport products) and adding margins of $800 and $8,000 associated with agricultural and manufacturing products.

However, the TLS on a product's vector includes, among other taxes, the nonrecoverable VAT associated with each product type. Other types of taxes may include excise taxes, customs duties, and import/export taxes. To interpret the values in the TLS on a product's vector (Figure 2.7), $3,545 is the nonrecoverable tax net of any subsidies imposed on all services and products purchased in the economy.

When TTM and TLS vectors are added to the vector for total domestic output and imports, the vector of total supply stated in purchasers' prices is derived. This will equal the vector of total use stated in purchasers' prices in a balanced supply and use system. In Figure 2.7, the total supply at the purchaser's prices equals $108,335.

Figure 2.7: The Supply Table

	AGR Sector	MFG Sector	SER Sector	Total domestic output at BP	M	Total supply at BP	Valuation		Total supply at PP
		Production matrix					TTM	TLS	
AGR Product	5,900	30	0	5,930	1,800	7,730	800	–	8,530
MFG Product	100	15,000	70	15,170	20,000	35,170	8,000	2,058	45,228
SER Product	150	560	55,410	56,120	5,770	61,890	(8,800)	1,487	54,577
Output at BP	**6,150**	**15,590**	**55,480**	**77,220**	**27,570**	**104,790**	**–**	**3,545**	**108,335**

AGR = agriculture; BP = basic prices; M = imports; MFG = manufacturing; PP = purchaser's prices; SER = services; TLS = taxes less subsidies on products; TTM = trade and transport margins.
Source: Authors.

---

9   In some SUTs, there are also margins in the financial sector from the insurance costs paid on products while in transit.

The Use Table

The use table (Figure 2.8) shows the use of goods and services by product and by type of use (intermediate consumption, final consumption, gross fixed capital formation, changes in inventories, and exports), with products and components of value-added as row headers and industries and type of use as column headers (European Commission 2008).[10] The use table also shows a vector referred to as the gross value-added (GVA), which is simply the difference between the value of output and intermediate consumption. GVA is further subdivided across its elements, which are compensation to employees, gross operating surplus, gross mixed income, and taxes on production (United Nations 2010).

To read the use table in Figure 2.8, say for agricultural products, the amount of $1,000 is the agricultural products used by the agriculture sector for production. Similarly, $2,500 and $410 are the amounts of agricultural products used respectively by the manufacturing and the services sectors in their production. Reading further through the row of agricultural products, households consumed $2,200, industries invested $640 (e.g., in the form of biological assets such as livestock) and $85 remained in inventory, and $1,695 were exported.

Figure 2.8: The Use Table

	AGR Sector	MFG Sector	SER Sector	Total IC	Final consumption HH	Final consumption NPISH	Final consumption Gov	GFCF	CII	X	Total use at PP
	IC matrix							Final demand matrix			
AGR Product	1,000	2,500	410	**3,910**	2,200	-	-	640	85	1,695	**8,530**
MFG Product	1,400	5,000	8,900	**15,300**	20,000	-	-	2,800	70	7,058	**45,228**
SER Product	500	1,790	15,070	**17,360**	13,080	240	6,480	7,840	-	9,577	**54,577**
Subtotal	**2,900**	**9,290**	**24,380**	**36,570**	**35,280**	**240**	**6,480**	**11,280**	**155**	**18,330**	**108,335**
GVA	3,250	6,300	31,100	**40,650**							
Output at BP	**6,150**	**15,590**	**55,480**	**77,220**							

AGR = agriculture; BP = basic prices; CII = changes in inventory; GFCF = gross fixed capital formation; Gov = government; GVA = gross value-added; HH = households; IC = intermediate consumption; MFG = manufacturing; NPISH = nonprofit institution serving households; PP = purchaser's prices; SER = services; X = exports.
Source: Authors.

[10] Notable in Figure 2.7 and Figure 2.8, the total supply and use at purchaser's prices is equal (balanced) for each product. Likewise, the output of each sector at basic prices presented in the SUTs are balanced.

Put another way, the use table shows (i) the input purchases of sectors within the intermediate consumption matrix and changes in the inventory vector, (ii) the capital purchases of industries within the gross fixed capital formation vector, and (iii) the final consumption of households, nonprofit institutions, and government within the final demand matrix. Providing the purchase details within an economy makes the use table an attractive tool to derive not just the amount of nonrecoverable VAT paid in the economy but also the structure of VAT payments by product and purchaser (i.e., the VAT valuation matrix). Therefore, the NAS-VAT model refers to the use table as its primary data source in estimating VAT on products.

Unlike the supply table, the use table does not explicitly indicate the amount of taxes paid for each product. Rather, nonrecoverable taxes are embedded within each use data because the use table is stated in purchaser's prices. In other words, both the intermediate consumption matrix and the final demand matrix incorporate nonrecoverable taxes absorbed, margins, and any transport charges paid by the purchaser within the amount of the product used.

Value-Added Tax Valuation Matrix

In the VAT valuation matrix (Figure 2.9), the total nonrecoverable VAT absorbed by VAT-exempt producers equals $620, while the nonrecoverable VAT absorbed by households equals $2,925.

Figure 2.9 shows the VAT embedded in the purchaser's price of each product used in the economy and takes the dimension of the use table. Taking the sum of the columns along the rows of the VAT valuation matrix yields the nonrecoverable VAT

Figure 2.9: Value-Added Tax Valuation Matrix

	AGR Sector	MFG Sector	SER Sector	Total VAT borne by producer	VAT on final consumption			GFCF	CII	X	VAT on products
					HH	NPISH	Gov				
AGR Product	–	–	–	–	–	–	–	–	–	–	–
MFG Product	119	1	170	290	1,769	–	–	–	–	–	2,058
SER Product	43	0	287	330	1,157	–	–	–	–	–	1,487
Subtotal	162	1	457	620	2,925	–	–	–	–	–	3,545
GVA	–	–	–	–							
Output at BP	128	1	361	620							

AGR = agriculture; CII = changes in inventory; GFCF = gross fixed capital formation; Gov = government; GVA = gross value-added; HH = households; MFG = manufacturing; NPISH = nonprofit institution serving households; SER = services; VAT = value-added tax; X = exports.
Source: Authors.

on products ($0, $2,058, $1,487), which should be parallel to the TLS on the products vector in the supply table (Figure 2.7). In Figure 2.9, the total nonrecoverable VAT absorbed by VAT-exempt producers equals $620, while the nonrecoverable VAT absorbed by households equals $2,925.

The NAS-VAT model provides a theoretically consistent methodology to extract the nonrecoverable VAT from the use table. Among other uses, the VAT valuation matrix is a vital input to transform the SUT into an input-output table.

Types of Output

Two main output types are included in the SUTs: market output and nonmarket output. The market output consists of output intended to be transacted in the market (e.g., products sold at economically significant prices, products bartered, products used for payments in kind, and products added to inventories intended for sale in the market). It includes production intended for own final consumption or own gross fixed capital formation. Nonmarket output consists of output by unincorporated enterprises owned by households and output by establishments owned by government units and nonprofit institutions (NPIs).[11] It includes those provided to households or the community as a whole for free or at economically insignificant prices (European Commission 2008).

As VAT is chargeable only on market sales of goods and services, only market output is within reach of value-added taxation. In addition, in most (if not all) jurisdictions, nonmarket sales at economically insignificant prices are VAT-exempt. Thus, the nonmarket output of the general government and NPI are either provided for free or at a nominal fee and are VAT-exempt.[12] For VAT computation purposes, the government and NPIs are regarded as the final consumer of the inputs used to produce the products they provide to households or the community on a nonmarket basis (Ebrill et al. 2001). Similarly, the nonmarket output of unincorporated enterprises, such as those owned by households, are excluded in the calculation for VAT when it is finally consumed, either through final consumption or gross fixed capital formation.

While the output of nonmarket producers (unincorporated enterprises owned by households, government, and NPIs) is not covered by the VAT system, nonmarket producers nonetheless pay VAT through their market purchases of inputs to nonmarket production. Not having any output VAT, the nonmarket producers absorb the input VAT on their purchases.

---

[11] Market output by unincorporated enterprises owned by households may still be treated in the same way as nonmarket output because sales are not made in the ordinary course of business. Sales not made in the ordinary course of business are typically not covered by the VAT system.

[12] The VAT exemption of the output of the general government is also consistent with value-added tax concepts, where goods and services sold by public (government) and private providers are exempted from VAT. This is to minimize further distortion of competition between the two providers (Ebrill et al. 2001). (Refer to footnote 2.)

The Non-Observed Economy

The non-observed economy (NOE) refers to all productive activities that may not be captured in the data sources for the compilation of national accounts statistics (United Nations Economic Commission for Europe 2008). The OECD describes five production activities that are typically missed by basic data collection: underground production, illegal production, informal sector production, household production for final use, and other deficiencies in data collection (Organisation for Economic Co-operation and Development 2002).[13] Despite being unobserved or concealed, national accounts statistics must impute and estimate the output from these activities to arrive at a comprehensive measure of GDP in the economy.

Recent literature estimates that the average size of the NOE in 158 economies from 1991 to 2015 was 31.9% of GDP (Medina and Schneider 2018).[14] Among select ADB DMCs, the size of the NOE as a percentage of GDP went down from an average of 38% in 2000 to 29.9% in 2015 (Figure 2.10-A). Meanwhile, there was considerable variability in the size of the NOE among ADB DMCs in 2015, with the lowest at 12.1% in the People's Republic of China and the highest at 53.1% in Georgia (Figure 2.10-B).

While underground production, illegal production, and informal sector production may be supplied to the economy as market output, the fact that the outputs are unobserved or concealed implies they are not registered with internal revenue authorities as taxpayers. Based on the concept of VAT non-registration, their output is offsetting within the stages of production and is ultimately decreased by the point at which it reaches the final consumer. The non-observed economic sector pays and absorbs VAT through their market purchases of inputs to production.

[13] Underground production refers to legal production activities that are concealed from public authorities to avoid compliance with several laws such as payment of taxes. Illegal production refers to production that is forbidden by law. Informal sector production involves units that typically operate on a small scale, at a low level of organization, and with little to no division between capital and labor as factors in production. Household production for final use includes the nonmarket output by unincorporated enterprises owned by households such as imputed rents of owner-occupied dwellings and paid domestic services (OECD 2002, UNECE 2007).

[14] All estimations were made using the Multiple Indicators Multiple Causes approach for comparability of estimates across economies (Medina and Schneider 2018).

Figure 2.10: Non-observed Economy in Select ADB Developing Member Countries

(A) Average Size of Non-Observed Economy in Select ADB DMCs, 2000–2015

(B) Size of Non-Observed Economy in Select ADB DMCs, 2015

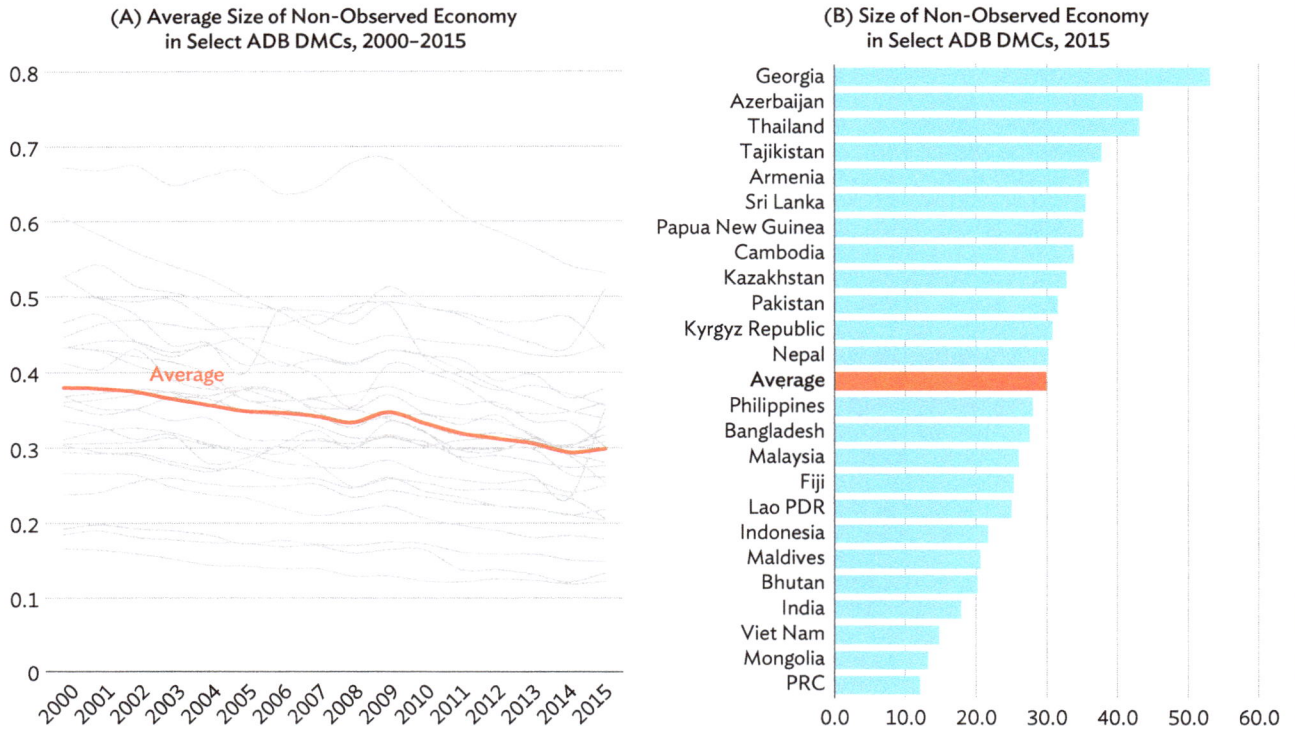

ADB = Asian Development Bank, DMC = developing member country, GDP = gross domestic product, Lao PDR = Lao People's Democratic Republic, PRC = People's Republic of China.

Note: The size of Select ADB Developing Member Countries (DMC) is computed as a share of GDP. Select ADB DMCs include Armenia, Azerbaijan, Bangladesh, Bhutan, Cambodia, People's Republic of China, Fiji, Georgia, India, Indonesia, Kazakhstan, Kyrgyz Republic, Lao People's Democratic Republic, Malaysia, Maldives, Mongolia, Nepal, Pakistan, Papua New Guinea, Philippines, Sri Lanka, Tajikistan, Thailand, and Viet Nam. The average is a simple unweighted average.

Source: Authors' calculations using data from the International Monetary Fund working paper: Shadow Economies Around the World: What Did We Learn Over the Last 20 Years? (Medina and Schneider 2018). https://www.imf.org/en/Publications/WP/Issues/2018/01/25/Shadow-Economies-Around-the-World-What-Did-We-Learn-Over-the-Last-20-Years-45583.

3

PUBLISHED ESTIMATION METHODOLOGIES

There are two approaches to estimating theoretical VAT collections: a consumption-based approach and a value-added approach. A consumption-based approach uses demand-side data to capture VAT borne by consumers in the economy. This approach is used by the HM Revenue and Customs (HMRC) of the UK in its VAT Total Theoretical Liability (VTTL) model and, as will be discussed in the subsequent section, the ADB National Accounts Statistics VAT (NAS-VAT) model. Meanwhile, a value-added approach mirrors the input-credit mechanism of the VAT, as adopted by the International Monetary Fund (IMF) Revenue Administration-Gap Analysis Program (RA-GAP) model for estimating VAT gaps.

Broadly, under a consumption-based approach, VAT is computed by taking the sum of VAT on intermediate consumption and VAT on final demand. In a value-added approach, VAT is derived by taking the sum of VAT on imports and the VAT on sold domestic output net of the VAT on related inputs. Regardless of the approach, both must arrive at the same theoretical VAT. Box 3.1 shows the equality derived using each approach.

3.1. HMRC VTTL Model

The HMRC VTTL model is intended to measure the VAT gap by estimating theoretical VAT collections and matching them with actual VAT collections. Given that the VTTL model follows a consumption-based approach, theoretical VAT is estimated by first identifying the total consumption of taxable goods and services from data sourced from the UK Office of National Statistics (ONS) national accounts macroeconomic aggregates. The total consumption of taxable products is broken down by commodity, and the corresponding commodity totals are multiplied by the applicable rate of VAT (0%, reduced, standard, or exempt) to determine the gross VTTL. To arrive at the net VTTL (i.e., theoretical VAT collection), gross VTTL is reduced by legitimate deductions such as refunds (primarily to government departments), expenditure on the output of businesses legitimately not registered for VAT (picked up in gross VTTL), and other deductions and tax reliefs (HMRC 2022). The VTTL model is summarized in Box 3.2.

Box 3.1: Equality of VAT Derived under a Consumption-Based Approach and a Value-Added Approach

The equivalence of the consumption-based approach and value-added approach for estimating VAT stems from the national accounts identity on the gross domestic product (GDP):

$$GDP = C + I + G + X - M$$
$$GDP = V + TLS$$

where C is household consumption, I is investment, G is government spending, X is exports, M is imports, V is gross value-added of all industries, and TLS is taxes less subsidies on products. Using this identity would mean that the sum of V and TLS must be equal to the sum of C, I, G, and X net of M.

$$V + TLS = C + I + G + X - M \text{ (Box 3.1 Equation 1)}$$

As the term (C + I + G + X − M) is stated gross of TLS, expressing it as net of TLS allows TLS to be cancelled on both sides of Equation 1. Suppose C_0, I_0, G_0, X_0, and M_0 are net values of TLS, then Equation 1 reduces to:

$$V = C_0 + I_0 + G_0 + X_0 - M_0 \text{ (Box 3.1 Equation 2)}$$

Using the consumption-based approach, theoretical VAT is computed by taking the sum of VAT on intermediate consumption (IC) and the VAT on final demand (FD). Note that FD comprises the final consumption of households (C) and government (G), investment (I), and exports (X). In equation form, this can be written as:

$$VAT_c = \tau IC_0 + \tau FD_0 = \tau IC_0 + \tau(C_0 + G_0 + I_0 + X_0) \text{ (Box 3.1 Equation 3)}$$

where VAT_c is the VAT derived using the consumption-based approach, τ is the standard rate of VAT, IC_0 is intermediate consumption net of TLS, and FD_0 is final consumption net of TLS.

Using the value-added approach, theoretical VAT is computed by taking the sum of VAT on imports and the VAT on sold domestic output (O) net of the VAT on related inputs (IC).[a] Because output less inputs is equivalent to gross value-added, $O_0 - IC_0$ is restated as V.

$$VAT_v = \tau M_0 + \tau(O_0 - IC_0) = \tau M_0 + \tau V \text{ (Box 3.1 Equation 4)}$$

where VAT_v is the VAT derived using the value-added approach and O_0 is domestic output net of TLS.

It can be shown that VAT_c is equivalent to VAT_v, as Equation 3 and Equation 4 will reduce to national accounts identity in Box 3.1 Equation 2.

$$VAT_c = VAT_v$$

$$\rightarrow \tau IC_0 + \tau(C_0 + G_0 + I_0 + X_0) = \tau M_0 + \tau V$$

Supposing standard VAT is universally applied (i.e., there are no exempt products and sectors), $\tau IC_0 = 0$, because input taxes can be refunded against the government. Thus,

$$\rightarrow \tau(C_0 + G_0 + I_0 + X_0) = \tau M_0 + \tau V$$

$$\rightarrow C_0 + G_0 + I_0 + X_0 = M_0 + V$$

$$\rightarrow V = C_0 + I_0 + G_0 + X_0 - M_0$$

$$\rightarrow V + TLS = C_0 + I_0 + G_0 + X_0 - M_0 + TLS$$

$$\rightarrow V + TLS = C + I + G + X - M$$

which is the national accounts identity.

[a] VAT on imports does not mean import tax.
Source: Authors.

Box 3.2: HM Revenue and Customs VAT Total Theoretical Liability Model

The HM Revenue and Customs (HMRC) Vat Total Theoretical Liability (VTTL) model estimates theoretical Value-added Tax (VAT) collections by subtracting legitimate deductions from gross VTTL. Gross VTTL is derived by applying the applicable rate of VAT (0%, reduced, standard, or exempt) to the corresponding total commodity expenditure of households (H), government (G), businesses making exempt supplies (E), household investment (HI), and nonprofit institutions serving households (N). Legitimate deductions are comprised of refunds, reliefs, hypothetical VAT from legitimately unregistered traders, and other deductions.[a]

$$\text{Net VTTL} = \sum_i (\tau_i\,\pi_i\,H_i + \tau_i\,\pi_i\,G_i + \tau_i\,\pi_i\,E_i + \tau_i\,\pi_i\,HI_i + \tau_i\,\pi_i\,N_i) - (\text{refunds} + \text{reliefs} + \text{hypothetical VAT from legitimately unregistered traders} + \text{other deductions})$$

(Box 3.2 Equation 1)

where τ_i is the applicable VAT rate on commodity i; π_i is the VAT fraction applicable to commodity i; and H_i, G_i, E_i, HI_i, and N_i are the respective expenditures of H, G, E, HI, and N of commodity i.

Expenditure data to compute net VTTL is mainly taken from the UK Office of National Statistics (ONS) national accounts macroeconomic aggregates. In regard to expenditure data, ONS national accounts are also used to estimate the VAT fraction. A VAT fraction is a nonnegative value not exceeding one, which refers to the proportion of commodity i that is taxable. The multiplicative product of the VAT fraction and the corresponding expenditure is the tax base subject to the standard or reduced rate.

In addition to ONS national accounts, data from the Department for Business, Energy and Industrial Strategy and the HMRC on the distribution of business revenue that falls below the VAT threshold supplements the estimation of nonrecoverable VAT from businesses making exempt supplies and the hypothetical VAT from legitimately unregistered traders.[b] For the remaining legitimate deductions, values are directly sourced from audited HMRC accounts data.

---

[a] Hypothetical VAT is the VAT that would have otherwise been imposed on legitimately unregistered traders if they were registered under the VAT system.
[b] Businesses with revenue that falls below the VAT threshold are commonly micro and small enterprises.
Source: HM Revenue and Customs. 2022. Measuring tax gaps 2021 edition – methodological annex. Retrieved from: https://www.gov.uk/government/statistics/measuring-tax-gaps/measuring-tax-gaps-2021-edition-methodological-annex#chapter-d-value-added-tax (accessed 8 February 2022).

While gross VTTL is estimated at the commodity expenditure level, legitimate deductions are not disaggregated at a matching level. Hence, the VTTL model, as it is, can only produce a single estimate of total theoretical VAT collections in the economy. Because only macroeconomic aggregates are used to estimate theoretical VAT, an estimate of nonrecoverable VAT on products consistent with the use-structure of the economy for a particular year may not be easily derived using the VTTL model.

3.2. IMF RA-GAP Model

In contrast to the HMRC VTTL model, which follows a consumption-based approach, the IMF RA-GAP model adopts a value-added approach. Thus, instead of using expenditure data, it uses data on imports and value-added data to estimate VAT (i.e., output minus inputs). The model mimics the input-credit mechanism that producers use to determine their individual tax liabilities. Given this, the estimated theoretical VAT equals the sum of the VAT paid on imports and the VAT payable by producers (output VAT less input VAT).

Like the NAS-VAT model, the principal data source of the RA-GAP model in estimating the theoretical VAT are supply and use tables (SUTs).[15] As SUTs offer a disaggregation of the economic transactions in the economy by product and by sector under a balanced supply and demand system, using it for estimating theoretical VAT ensures consistency of estimates for the associated market transactions. Box 3 summarizes the RA-GAP model.

Box 3.3: International Monetary Fund Revenue Administration-Gap Analysis Program Model

The International Monetary Fund Revenue Administration-Gap Analysis Program (IMF RA-GAP) model estimates theoretical Value-added Tax (VAT) collections (referred to as "potential VAT" in Hutton (2017) by taking the sum of VAT on imports and VAT on sold domestic output net of VAT on related inputs. Equations to estimate VAT on imports, VAT on sold domestic output, and VAT on related inputs are given shown in Equations 1 to 3.

Estimating VAT on imports (VAT_M) is straightforward. The commodity imports traded in the market are multiplied by the applicable VAT rate. Box 3 Equation 1 summarizes this.

$$VAT_M = \sum_i (M_i^s \times \tau_i) \qquad \textbf{(Box 3.3 Equation 1)}$$

where M_i^s is imports by sector s of commodity i; and is the VAT rate applicable to commodity i.

VAT on sold domestic output (VAT_O) is analogous to the output VAT described in Section 2. It is derived by multiplying sector output net of exports by the applicable VAT rate and the proportion of VAT-registered firms in a sector. It is imperative to only calculate output VAT on the portion of the sector that is VAT-registered because the non-registered portions are not expected by law to remit VAT.

$$VAT_O = \sum_i (O_i^s - X_i^s \times \tau_i \times r^s) \qquad \textbf{(Box 3.3 Equation 2)}$$

where O_i^s is the output of commodity i by sector s; X_i^s is the exports of commodity i by sector s; and r^s is the proportion of value-added in sector s produced by entities registered for VAT.

Meanwhile, VAT on related inputs (VAT_N) is analogous to input VAT described in Section 2. Related inputs comprise intermediate consumption and gross fixed capital formation. The sum of the related inputs is multiplied by the applicable VAT rate and by the proportion of VAT-registered firms in a sector. As with the computation of output VAT in Box 3 Equation 2, input VAT is likewise only computed for VAT-registered firms because only these entities are allowed to claim input tax credits (ITC). Inputs that are VAT-exempt must not be associated with an input VAT. General disallowances in claiming ITCs must also be considered (e.g., disallowance of ITC related to entertainment expenses in some jurisdictions).

$$VAT_N = \sum_i (N_i^s + I_i^s) \times \tau_i \times r^s \times (1 - e^s) \times \eta_i^s \qquad \textbf{(Box 3.3 Equation 3)}$$

where is N_i^s the intermediate consumption of commodity i by sector s; I_i^s is the gross fixed capital formation of commodity i by sector s; e^s is the proportion of output of sector s that is exempt; and η_i^s is the proportion of ITC for commodity by i sector s that is allowed to be claimed.

Equation 4 shows how potential VAT is derived in the IMF RA-GAP model.

$$\text{Potential VAT} = VAT_M + VAT_O - VAT_N \qquad \textbf{(Box 3.3 Equation 4)}$$

Source: Hutton 2017. The Revenue Administration—Gap Analysis Program: Model and Methodology for Value-Added Tax Gap Estimation. Technical Notes and Manuals. International Monetary Fund.

---

[15] Hutton (2017) refers to "theoretical VAT" as "potential VAT" in the RA-GAP model.

To better measure and understand the compliance gap and fit in the purpose of risk management, the IMF RA-GAP model breaks down the theoretical VAT by sector. This may not meet the needs of national accounts statistics compilation, which require the compilation of product-disaggregated nonrecoverable VAT.

To understand the difference between VAT payable by sector (IMF RA-GAP estimates) and the nonrecoverable VAT on products required in national accounts compilation (NAS-VAT estimates), Figure 3.1 shows the production stages and ultimate sale of commodity i. Commodity i is sold to the final consumer for $800, with the final consumer paying $880 ($800 cost of the commodity, $80 VAT, assuming a VAT rate of 10%). The $80 VAT paid on the final consumption of commodity i (red cell in Figure 3.1) is the nonrecoverable VAT on product i because it is not recovered as a tax credit. The $80 VAT is physically received by stage 5 producers but is actually payable to the government in stages by various producers (yellow cells in Figure 3.1). Such is the estimate by the IMF RA-GAP model.

Figure 3.1: Value-Added Tax Paid on Commodity i

	Stage 1	Stage 2	Stage 3	Stage 4	Stage 5	FC
Output sold from stage n to stage n+1	100	200	400	500	800	
Less: Cost of inputs of stage n from stage n-1	0	100	200	400	500	800
Value-added	100	100	200	100	300	
Output VAT	10	20	40	50	80	
Less: Input VAT	0	10	20	40	50	80
VAT payable to the government from stage n	10	10	20	10	30	

FC = final consumer.
Note: The assumption is that stage 1 only uses primary inputs (labor and capital). The standard rate of VAT is 10%. Output sold from stage n to stage n+1 is net of VAT. The amount paid on purchases by the final consumer is gross of VAT.

Total VAT payable in Figure 3.1 is equal to $80 ($10 + $10 + $20 + $10 + $30), which is exactly the nonrecoverable VAT on commodity i. The former is the estimate under a value-added approach (e.g., IMF RA-GAP model), while the latter is the estimate under a consumption-based approach (e.g., HMRC VTTL model, NAS-VAT model). This shows that, numerically, both approaches are conceptually the same and must yield the same theoretical VAT.

4

ADB NATIONAL ACCOUNTS STATISTICS VALUE-ADDED TAX MODEL

The existing published estimation methodologies (HMRC VTTL model and IMF RA-GAP model) are explicitly designed to derive a measure of the VAT gap in an economy. The HMRC VTTL model is designed to develop an aggregate measure of the VAT gap as it uses macroeconomic expenditure aggregates to estimate total theoretical VAT using the consumption-based approach. The IMF RA-GAP model also generates a measure of theoretical VAT but is disaggregated at the level of each sector's VAT payable using the SUTs.

Following the System of National Accounts (SNA), the compilation of national accounts statistics does not require the derivation of the VAT gap. Rather, it only requires the compilation of product-disaggregated nonrecoverable VAT (nonrecoverable VAT on products). Theoretical VAT derived using both the VTTL and the RA-GAP models do not fit national account requirements. The former does not meet the disaggregation level (it must be product level), while the latter is limited in reconciling the transactions between an economy's supply of products and its corresponding uses with consistent valuations. The NAS-VAT model addresses both limitations and results in an estimate of theoretical VAT that is disaggregated at the product level. The NAS-VAT model feeds into the quality check of the balance between a product's use in the economy with its corresponding supply at its final valuation. The model can also be used to derive a measure of the VAT gap at an aggregate level, which can serve a similar purpose as the VTTL and RA-GAP models if the related SUT has been compiled with reasonable accuracy.

4.1. The Policy Variables

The salient element of the NAS-VAT model is the policy variables, which are mainly characterized by the tax legislation and business surveys on VAT registration. Policy variables are aggregated into policy matrices, with each policy matrix describing the value-added taxability of commodity i used by any sector s or any final consumer k. Policy matrices take the dimension of the use table shown in Figure 2.8, excluding the rows and columns for subtotals and the row for gross value-added.

To set up the model, suppose in Country X there are m products and n industries. Let C be $m \times n$ an intermediate consumption matrix; Y be $m \times p$ a final demand matrix, where p refers to the number of final demand categories; and S be an $m \times n$ production matrix.[16] Let U be the country's $m \times (n + p)$ use matrix, comprising the matrix C in the first n columns and the matrix Y is the last p columns.

In this setup, the policy matrices will also take a dimension of $m \times (n + p)$. In Country X, policy variables ϕ_{ij} (nontax object), ϵ_{ij} (VAT-exempt), ζ_{ij} (zero-rated), ι_{ij} and (input tax credit) are aggregated in policy matrices Φ, E, Z, and H, respectively. Subscript $i = 1,..., m$ refers to the products, $j = 1,..., n + p$ and refers to the users (i.e., sectors plus the final demand categories) in the use table. Table 4.1 describes policy variables and policy matrices in any country x.[17]

Table 4.1: Description of Policy Matrices in Any Country X

Policy Matrix	Short Name	Policy Variables	Description
Φ	Nontax Object Matrix	ϕ_{ij}	This matrix contains the proportions of the elements of the use table, which are not taxable objects, such as imputed use of ownership of dwellings, changes in inventories, and other nonmarket transactions. Each policy variable ϕ_{ij} refers to the proportion of product used by user j (either sector or final demand category) that is not a taxable object.
E	VAT-Exempt Matrix	ϵ_{ij}	This matrix contains the proportions of the product used that are VAT-exempt based on the tax legislation. Each policy variable ϵ_{ij} refers to the proportion of product i used by user j (either sector or final demand category) that is VAT-exempt.
Z	Zero-Rated Matrix	ζ_{ij}	This matrix contains the proportions of the product used that are subject to 0% VAT (i.e., zero-rated) based on the tax legislation. Each policy variable ζ_{ij} refers to the proportion of product i used by user j (either sector or final demand category) that is zero-rated.
H	Input Tax Credit Matrix	ι_{ij}	This matrix contains the proportions of the industry that can deduct input taxes on their purchases against the output taxes on their sales. Each policy variable ι_{ij} refers to the proportion of product i used by user j (either sector or final demand category) with corresponding input tax that can be claimed as credits.

Source: Authors.

[16] Final demand categories include household final consumption, final consumption of nonprofit institutions serving households, general government final consumption, gross fixed capital formation, and changes in inventories. The number of final demand items may vary from country-to-country depending on the disaggregation of each item. For example, some economies may choose to present general government final consumption (GGFC) as collective GGFC and individual GGFC, while some present one aggregated vector for GGFC.

[17] Note that Table 4.1 only includes the most basic policy variables. Other jurisdictions have more complex taxation regimes, such as additional provisions for reduced rates, rebates, presumptive input VAT, and transitional input VAT among others. Additional policy variables need to be defined to accommodate these nuances.

The input tax credit matrix $\mathbf{H}$ can be estimated given $m \times n$ the production matrix $\mathbf{S}$ and the policy matrix $\mathbf{E}$. Both matrices are used to estimate the VAT-exempt supply sold in each sector that is not allowed to recover input VAT as tax credits.

Because input tax credits only apply to market producers, $\mathbf{H}$ is partitioned to distinguish producers and final consumers. Let $\mathbf{H}$ contain two submatrices: $\mathbf{H_C}$ ($m \times n$) and $\mathbf{H_Y}$ ($m \times p$). Each submatrix refers to the input tax credit submatrix applicable to the intermediate consumption matrix $\mathbf{C}$ and the final demand matrix $\mathbf{Y}$, respectively. In general, $\mathbf{H_Y}$ is a matrix of zeroes because final consumers cannot claim input tax credits.[18]

Suppose there is no nonmarket production or non-observed economy. Suppose further there is no revenue threshold, and all VAT-exempt products are those stated in the legislation.[19] To estimate $\mathbf{H_C}$, a corresponding $m \times n$ submatrix $\mathbf{E_C}$ is extracted from the VAT-exempt matrix $\mathbf{E}$. Matrix $\mathbf{E_C}$ contains the proportion of each product i used by each industry s that is VAT-exempt. Let $\mathbf{h'}$ be a $1 \times n$ vector containing the proportion of value-added-taxable supply per sector. Equation 1 shows how $\mathbf{h'}$ can be derived using the production matrix $\mathbf{S}$ and the VAT-exempt submatrix $\mathbf{E_C}$.

$$\mathbf{h'} = \mathbf{i'} - \frac{\mathbf{i'}\,(\mathbf{S} \times \mathbf{E_C})}{\mathbf{i'}\,\mathbf{S}} \qquad \textbf{Equation 1}$$

Note: $\times$ is the Hadamard product operator (i.e., the operator for element-by-element multiplication). The term $\frac{\mathbf{i'}(\mathbf{S} \times \mathbf{E_C})}{\mathbf{i'}\,\mathbf{S}}$ contains the proportion of VAT-exempt supply per sector j.

Each element h_j of $\mathbf{h'}$ is the proportion of value-added-taxable supply per sector j that can claim input tax credits. The row vector $\mathbf{h'}$ will make up the $\mathbf{H_C}$ matrix by taking the Kronecker product of the $m \times 1$ unit vector $\mathbf{i}_m$ and $\mathbf{h'}$.

$$\mathbf{H_C} = \mathbf{i}m \otimes \mathbf{h'} \qquad \textbf{Equation 1.1}$$

Note: $\otimes$ is the Kronecker product operator. This operation essentially duplicates the vector in rows.

To construct the $m \times (n + p)$ input tax credit matrix $\mathbf{H}$, $\mathbf{H_C}$, and $\mathbf{H_Y}$ are appended, with the $\mathbf{H_C}$ submatrix representing the first n columns and the $\mathbf{H_Y}$ representing the last p columns. This process is depicted in Figure 4.1.

[18] In particular, $\mathbf{H_Y}$ does not apply to the vector of gross fixed capital formation. Because the vector of gross fixed capital formation may be disaggregated across investing sectors (becoming the gross fixed capital formation matrix), the input tax credit submatrix applicable to intermediate consumption $\mathbf{H_C}$ is also applicable to the gross fixed capital formation matrix. For simplicity when discussing the NAS-VAT model, it is assumed that all input VAT on gross fixed capital formation can be claimed as tax credits, hence, $\mathbf{H_Y} = [0]$.

[19] To minimize the administrative burden on micro and small enterprises, jurisdictions typically legislate a revenue threshold below which registration in the VAT system is not mandatory. If these producers opt to not register, then their sales, regardless of the product, will be VAT-exempt, and they will not be allowed to claim input tax credits on their purchases.

Figure 4.1: Construction of the Input Tax Credit Matrix $\mathbf{H}$

$$\mathbf{H} = \boxed{\begin{array}{c|c} \mathbf{H_C} = im \otimes h' & \mathbf{H_Y} \end{array}}$$

$$\mathbf{H} = $$

h_1	h_2	$\cdots$	h_j	$\cdots$	h_n	0	0	$\cdots$	0
h_1	h_2	$\cdots$	h_j	$\cdots$	h_n	0	0	$\ddots$	0
$\vdots$	$\vdots$	$\ddots$	$\vdots$	$\ddots$	$\vdots$	$\vdots$	$\vdots$	$\ddots$	$\vdots$
h_1	h_2	$\cdots$	h_j	$\cdots$	h_n	0	0	$\cdots$	0

Source: Authors.

4.2. The Taxable Proportion

The taxable proportion of a product i is the portion of its value that is ultimately taxed. In other words, it is the proportion of the product value used by final consumers and firms with VAT-exempt supplies. Given the policy variables described in Table 4.1, the taxable proportion of product i consumed by user j, π_{ij}, could be derived by determining the proportion of the product i that is a taxable object $(1 - \phi_{ij})$, is neither VAT-exempt $(1 - \epsilon_{ij})$ nor zero-rated $(1 - \zeta_{ij})$, and has input VAT that cannot be claimed as tax credits $(1 - \iota_{ij})$. The same is given by Equation 2, which aggregates to an $m \times (n + p)$ matrix Π.

$$\pi_{ij} = (1 - \phi_{ij}) \cdot (1 - \epsilon_{ij}) \cdot (1 - \zeta_{ij}) \cdot (1 - \iota_{ij}) \qquad \textbf{Equation 2}$$

4.3. The Nonrecoverable Rate

The VAT of each product i consumed by user j can be estimated naively by multiplying the corresponding taxable proportion by the value of the product used and the standard rate of VAT, τ. Doing so will result in less accurate VAT estimates because the use table is compiled in prices that are in contrast with the tax base. The use table is compiled in purchaser's prices, which includes margins and nonrecoverable taxes, while the VAT base typically refers to the market price but excludes any nonrecoverable VAT.

Therefore, there is a need to isolate the nonrecoverable VAT embedded within the purchaser's prices to arrive at more accurate estimates of VAT. To do so, instead of multiplying the standard VAT rate by the taxable proportion of the product, the nonrecoverable rate is used instead. Each nonrecoverable rate r_{ij} is given by Equation 3, and aggregates to an $m \times (n + p)$ matrix $\mathbf{R}$.

$$r_{ij} = \frac{\tau\pi_{ij}}{1 + \tau\pi_{ij}}$$ **Equation 3**

Note: τ is the standard rate of value-added tax.

4.4. Value-Added Tax on Products

The VAT embedded in the purchaser's price of each product, t_{ij}, is derived by multiplying the use of product i consumed by user j, u_{ij}, by the corresponding nonrecoverable rate, r_{ij}. Equation 4 shows the computation of the theoretical VAT valuation matrix, $\mathbf{T}$.

$$\mathbf{T} = \mathbf{U} \times \mathbf{R}$$ **Equation 4**

Note: is the Hadamard product operator (i.e., the operator for element-by-element multiplication).

The $\mathbf{T}$ matrix can be partitioned into an $(m \times n)$ matrix $\mathbf{T}_C$ and an $m \times p$ matrix $\mathbf{T}_Y$, which corresponds to the VAT from the intermediate consumption matrix $\mathbf{C}$ and the final demand matrix $\mathbf{Y}$, respectively. Figure 4.2 is a visual representation of the theoretical VAT valuation matrix.

The theoretical VAT absorbed by each VAT-exempt sector from their inputs is given by the $1 \times n$ row vector $\mathbf{i}'\,\mathbf{T}_C$, and the total theoretical VAT borne by the producers is represented by the scalar $\mathbf{i}'\,\mathbf{T}_C\mathbf{i}$. The VAT borne by producers represents the input taxes they were not able to credit because of the VAT exemption of their sales. Meanwhile, theoretical VAT paid by each final consumer on their purchases is represented in the $1 \times p$ row vector $\mathbf{i}'\,\mathbf{T}_Y$. Theoretical VAT on each product is derived from the $m \times 1$ column vector $\mathbf{T}_C\mathbf{i} + \mathbf{T}_Y\mathbf{i}$. Finally, total theoretical VAT in the economy is equal to $\mathbf{i}'\,\mathbf{T}_C\mathbf{i} + \mathbf{i}'\,\mathbf{T}_Y\mathbf{i} \equiv \Psi$.

Figure 4.2: Theoretical Value-Added Tax Valuation Matrix

Item	I1	I2	I3	Total VAT borne by producer	Final consumption			GFCF	CII	X	Total VAT by product
					HH	NPISH	Gov				
P1											
P2		T_C		T_Ci			T_Y				$T_Ci + T_Yi$
P3											
GVA	0	0	0	0							0
Total VAT by user		$i'T_C$	$i'T_Ci$				$i'T_Y$				$i'T_Ci + i'T_Yi$

CII = changes in inventory; GFCF = gross fixed capital formation; Gov = government; GVA = gross value-added; HH = households; NPISH = nonprofit institution serving households; VAT = value-added tax; X = exports.
Source: Authors.

4.5. Accrued Value-Added Tax

For national accounts statistics, VAT on products are compiled on an accrual basis, that is, in the same period when the transactions that create the liabilities to pay taxes occur. The amounts compiled and recorded as VAT for national accounts statistics are those due for payment and are evidenced by VAT assessments. This means that national accounts statistics do not impute values for missing taxes because of the absence of VAT assessments (United Nations 2010).

Accrued VAT can be compiled from internal revenue data, but generally at a highly aggregated level. This is why there is a need to estimate VAT on a product level (to generate a vector for taxes less subsidies on products) and VAT on a product-sector level (to generate a VAT valuation matrix), as discussed in earlier sections.

Equation 4 results in theoretical VAT due in the economy for a given period, which is derived from all contemporaneous transactions in the use matrix U. Therefore, total theoretical VAT is associated with transactions that occur in the same period when the liabilities to pay taxes accrue. However, there is no assurance that all values in the use matrix U are evidenced by VAT assessments, for example, when a VAT payer inadvertently or willfully conceals their sales from revenue authorities. While VAT may be accrued from such transactions, it will not be evidenced by VAT assessments. Hence, in cases when total theoretical VAT is not equal to total accrued VAT from internal revenue data (henceforth 'actual VAT'), there is a need to recalculate the VAT on products such that it is only compiled for VAT that is both due for payment and is evidenced by VAT assessments, as required by the system of national accounts.

4.6. Compiling the Actual Value-Added Tax Valuation Matrix

Total theoretical VAT in the economy will rarely be equal to the actual VAT. The positive difference between the two is the VAT gap (VG) given by Equation 5. VG may arise from administrative leakages or evasion. Moreover, VG also captures any inadequacies in the compilation of the supply and use tables. The NAS-VAT model does not formally characterize the nature of the VG and generally interprets it as the excess of theoretical VAT over actual VAT. Nonetheless, as supply and use tables converge to the actual economic system, the measure of VG approaches a measure of the efficiency of VAT administration.

An alternative to the VG is the Theoretical VAT Ratio (TVR), which is derived by taking the ratio of the actual VAT and theoretical VAT (Equation 6). Because it is unitless, the TVR is a better indicator than VG to assess two things. First, the TVR can signal potential inconsistencies in the supply and use system. Because actual VAT will always be less than or equal to the theoretical VAT, TVR will always be less than or equal to one. If the TVR turns out to be greater than one (or if TVR is too low), it prompts further investigation of either the SUTs or the actual (accrued) VAT. An assessment of the reasonableness of the TVR is best done in conjunction with revenue authorities.

Second, once inconsistencies in the supply and use system are resolved, the TVR can be used as a measure of how well VAT revenue was collected, compared to what could have been raised in theory. The TVR is also a better measure than the VG for temporal and spatial comparisons.

$$VG = \text{Theoretical VAT} - \text{Actual VAT}, VG \geq 0 \qquad \textbf{Equation 5}$$

$$TVR = \frac{\text{Actual VAT}}{\text{Theoretical VAT}}, 0 < TVR \leq 1 \qquad \textbf{Equation 6}$$

For the purpose of national accounts compilation, the general assumption is that the VG across products used in the economy is homogeneous. Thus, the structure of is adopted to compile the actual VAT valuation matrix, and the matrix that will comprise the actual VAT valuation matrix is given by Equation 7. Appendix 1 presents a simple illustration of the NAS-VAT model using a simple SUT structure.

$$T^A = TVR \cdot T \qquad \textbf{Equation 7}$$

5 VALUE-ADDED TAX ON PRODUCTS IN THE SUPPLY AND USE TABLE

To generate high quality and reliable national accounts statistics for evidence-based policymaking, ADB provides technical assistance to national statistics offices, primarily in the construction of SUTs. Each component of the SUT must be consistent with the supply and demand of goods and services in the economy. Therefore, as a component of the SUT, VAT on products must be consistent with the supply and demand system, the prevailing tax legislation, the input-credit mechanism, and the system of national accounts guidance for compilation. The NAS-VAT model is designed to generate estimates consistent with these elements.

In practice, the NAS-VAT model is applied in conjunction with balancing the SUTs. The SUTs are designed such that all products supplied are exactly equal to the products used in the economy. When SUTs are initially compiled, product supply and use generally do not equal one another, and it is only after rounds of reconciliation are they balanced (i.e., supply = use).

The use table encapsulates how each commodity is consumed by industries to produce a new commodity. As previously discussed, policy matrices are prepared by distinguishing which of the products used are not taxable, VAT-exempt, or zero-rated. Most industries would have redeemed the input tax paid through the output tax imposed on each sale. Some users enjoy rebates or special accommodations. In some economies, VAT is not collected from government spending. A rebate is provided at the point of sale. A taxable proportion is calculated to represent the share of each transaction taxed. Subsequently, a nonrecoverable rate per transaction of each user (intermediate or final) is estimated by considering the taxable proportion and standard VAT rate. Ultimately, the supply and use framework facilitates the estimation of the VAT by multiplying the nonrecoverable rate to each use at the product level by each industry or final user. The row sum of this matrix forms part of the initial estimate of the VAT on the products column vector to be integrated into the supply table.

The NAS-VAT model helps uncover inconsistencies between supply and use if applied iteratively, beginning with a reasonably balanced SUT. The initial estimate of the vector of VAT on products is plugged into the vector of taxes less subsidies (TLS) on products in the supply table. The new total product supply is compared with total product use (total supply at basic prices + trade and transport margins + TLS on products, Figure 2.7). Consequently, plugging the calculated VAT on products and its corresponding comparison into the total product use updates the product discrepancies to varying degrees. Discrepancies for some products minimize, while for others, the distance widens between the estimated supply compared to use. Any inconsistency revealed by analyzing the tax imposed on a product level or at the industry and sector levels will be addressed by the national accountant and tax specialist using knowledgeable assessments via independent data sources and research. These insights can guide the refinement of the use table and the VAT matrix.

After product supply and use are corrected to reflect more accurate values, the reasonably balanced SUT is used to re-estimate nonrecoverable VAT on products using the NAS-VAT model for another round. The resulting vector of VAT on products is again plugged into the supply table, and the new total product supply is again compared with total product use. If there are still inconsistencies between supply and use, another round of knowledgeable assessments and rebalancing are employed by the national accountant.

Updating the TLS vector does not impact any of the calculations regarding the policy variables. In all these variables, only the domestic production and imports vector regions of the supply table are being referenced in the calculations. The changes in the valuation margins, including the updated TLS vector, are isolated in the iterative recalculation of VAT estimates through the SUT framework. However, the process of updating the VAT estimates is integral to the reconciliation between the supply table and the use table. Any adjustment in either table due to the reconciliation process necessitates updating the VAT estimates. For instance, an adjustment in a product in the use table to balance with its corresponding row in the supply table implies that the related VAT should be re-estimated.

The process of re-estimation, knowledgeable assessments, and rebalancing continues until there are no more inconsistencies or discrepancies between supply and use. In this scenario, the estimate of VAT on products would fit perfectly in the supply table and would not introduce any new discrepancy between supply and use. Figure 5.1 depicts the iterative process involving the model and the SUT rebalancing.

Figure 5.1: NAS-VAT Model and SUT Rebalancing Iterative Process

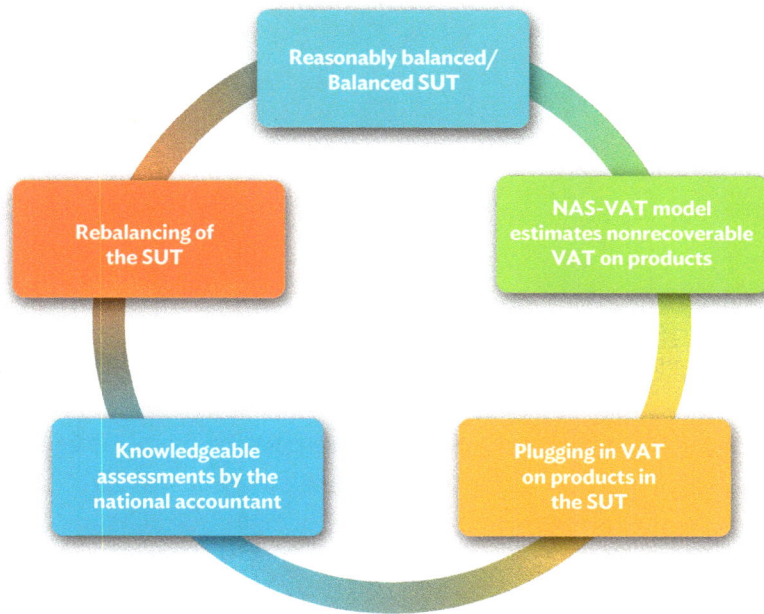

NAS-VAT model = Asian Development Bank National Accounts Statistics Value-Added Tax model; SUT = supply and use table; VAT = value-added tax.
Note: The iterative process stops when there are no more inconsistencies between supply and use and when the estimate of nonrecoverable VAT on products does not introduce any new discrepancies between supply and use. In this scenario, the SUT is perfectly balanced.
Source: Authors.

6 APPLICATIONS

As part of generating reliable national accounts statistics in ADB developing member countries (DMCs), nonrecoverable VAT on products was estimated using the NAS-VAT model for Armenia, Kazakhstan, and Uzbekistan.[20]

A generally balanced table was used because the simultaneous estimation of VAT and the development of the SUT help the national accountant derive reasonably accurate VAT estimates and ultimately balance the SUTs as part of the iterative process in Figure 5.1.[21] For Armenia, the experimental 2017–2018 SUT was used to estimate nonrecoverable VAT on products; for Kazakhstan, the years covered were 2017–2019; and for Uzbekistan, the years 2016–2019. External data sources were also used to disaggregate products and sectors in the experimental SUT when they were not as disaggregated as the provisions on products and sectors in the tax legislation. A complete list of data sources used in the estimation is provided in Appendix 3.

Subsidiary to the process of constructing the actual VAT valuation matrix, statistics on the VG and the TVR are determined. Table 6.2 shows the VG and the TVR for Armenia in 2017-2018, Kazakhstan in 2017–2019, and Uzbekistan in 2016–2019. As discussed, the VG and the TVR may permit the examination of the efficiency of VAT administration and compliance over time. However, one can do so only if the SUTs are compiled with sufficient accuracy.

Table 6.1: VAT Gap and Theoretical VAT Ratio

Item	Armenia 2017	Armenia 2018	Kazakhstan 2017	Kazakhstan 2018	Kazakhstan 2019	Uzbekistan 2016	Uzbekistan 2017	Uzbekistan 2018	Uzbekistan 2019
Total theoretical VAT	528,620	547,689	2,608,172	3,065,291	3,299,455	20,325,945	24,068,648	34,914,442	43,374,529
Total actual VAT	406,685	438,219	1,664,699	2,034,314	2,693,127	11,891,644	14,685,796	27,876,532	33,809,800
VAT gap	**122,037**	**109,470**	**943,473**	**1,030,977**	**606,328**	**8,434,300**	**9,382,852**	**6,037,910**	**9,564,729**
Theoretical VAT ratio	**76.9%**	**80.0%**	**63.8%**	**66.4%**	**81.6%**	**58.5%**	**61.0%**	**82.2%**	**77.9%**

VAT = value-added tax.
Note: Total theoretical VAT, total actual VAT, and VAT gap figures are in millions of local currency. Local currency in Armenia is AMD, Kazakhstan is KZT, and Uzbekistan is UZS.
Source: Estimates using the NAS-VAT model.

---

[20] Data is generated by ADB for research purposes based on publicly available information, and from the research work arising from the technical assistance to the developing member countries.

[21] The estimation of VAT on products is integral to the compilation of the SUT. A series of estimations and re-estimations of VAT is accomplished as the SUT evolves during the balancing process until the SUT is balanced (i.e., supply and demand in the economy are balanced) and the VAT computed converges to a more refined estimate.

There is an assumption that if there are no changes in the tax regime and implementation of VAT administration, the gap between the theoretical VAT and the actual collection would close in over time. While there were only two data points, this assumption was observed in Armenia where the TVR increased between 2017 and 2018. In Kazakhstan, TVR consistently increased between 2017 and 2019, even with the introduction of the new tax legislation implemented in 2018. TVR in 2019 was significantly higher compared to 2017 and 2018, which may be partly attributable to the increasing administrative efficiency of the VAT control accounts since 2018 and the decline in the output of illegal activity. In Uzbekistan, TVR increased between 2016 and 2019 but decreased between 2018 and 2019, possibly attributable to adjustments to taxpayer compliance in the 2019 tax reform that reduced the VAT rate from 20% to 15%.

The observations on the evolution of the VG and TVR in Armenia, Kazakhstan, and Uzbekistan are not conclusive. Apart from the need for consistent SUTs over time, there is also a need for more rigorous testing to tease out the effects of changes in the VAT regime on VG and TVR.

7 CONCLUSION

The compilation of SUTs provides opportunities to reconcile data from varying statistical sources and to reveal characteristics that serve analytical purposes. As an underlying method for compiling SUTs, the NAS-VAT model also promotes similar opportunities. It allows for comingling tax legislation and the supply and use framework to generate a theoretically consistent measure of VAT, producing insightful statistics useful for national statisticians in generating consistent statistics and for policymakers designing fiscal policies.

Once the SUTs are compiled with sufficient accuracy, the VAT gap and theoretical VAT ratio provide measures of the transactions included in the SUTs but are not evidenced by VAT assessments. Therefore, they may be used as statistics that measure the strength of VAT administration and assess the impacts of tax reforms on tax revenue collections over time.

Alternative regime scenarios (i.e., broad-based versus narrow-based) may be tested using the NAS-VAT model via modifications to policy matrices. Because it is a simple model, policymakers may easily use it to determine the implications on total theoretical VAT (increase or decrease) given regime changes. However, more comprehensive analyses may be conducted when the model results are extended to a computable general equilibrium analysis.

While the demand for detailed and disaggregated data is high for the application of the model, the methodology is relatively simple and easy to apply once its salient elements have been defined (the policy variables, the taxable proportion, and the non-recoverable rate). Its consistency with the supply and use system makes it highly attractive to policymakers trained to rely on data and evidence to generate meaningful policies.

ILLUSTRATION OF THE NAS-VAT MODEL

The following constitutes Country A's supply and use tables (SUTs). The national accountant knows that the actual accrued value-added tax (VAT) is $3,545.
In Country A, this is the sole component of taxes less subsidies (TLS) on products in the supply table. However, the national accountant does not know how the actual VAT is disaggregated across products, which is required to complete and balance the SUTs.

Supply Table

Item	AGR Sector	MFG Sector	SER Sector	Total Domestic Output at BP	M	Total Supply at BP	Valuation TTM	Valuation TLS	Total Supply at PP
AGR product	5,900	30	0	5,930	1,800	7,730	800	?	
MFG product	100	15,000	70	15,170	20,000	35,170	8,000	?	
SER product	150	560	55,410	56,120	5,770	61,890	(8,800)	?	
Output at BP	6,150	15,590	55,480	77,220	27,570	104,790	–	3,545	

AGR = agriculture, BP = basic prices, M = imports, MFG = manufacturing, PP = purchaser's prices, SER = services, TLS = taxes less subsidies on products, TTM = trade and transport margins, VAT = value-added tax.
Source: Authors.

Use Table

Item	AGR Sector	MFG Sector	SER Sector	Total IC	Final consumption HH	NPISH	Gov	GFCF	CII	X	Total use at PP
AGR product	1,000	2,500	410	3,910	2,200	–	–	640	85	1,695	8,530
MFG product	1,400	5,000	8,900	15,300	20,000	–	–	2,800	70	7,058	45,228
SER product	500	1,790	15,070	17,360	13,080	240	6,480	7,840	–	9,577	54,577
Subtotal	2,900	9,290	24,380	36,570	35,280	240	6,480	11,280	155	18,330	108,335
GVA	3,250	6,300	31,100	40,650							
Output at BP	6,150	15,590	55,480	77,220							

AGR = agriculture, BP = basic prices, CII = changes in inventory, GFCF = gross fixed capital formation, Gov = government, GVA = gross value-added, HH = households, IC = intermediate consumption, MFG = manufacturing, NPISH = nonprofit institution serving households, PP = purchaser's prices, SER = services, X = exports.
Source: Authors.

Given the use table, the national accountant can use the NAS-VAT model to estimate the structure of the VAT on the products vector and the VAT valuation matrix. To further illustrate how the model works, assume the following provisions on Economy A's tax legislation and external statistics:

1. All agricultural products are VAT-exempt.
2. All outputs of nonprofit institution serving households (NPISH) and the government are nonmarket production.
3. Nonmarket output of NPISH and government is 20% of services.
4. Exports are zero-rated.
5. All capital formation is by firms that can claim input tax credits.
6. Standard rate of VAT is 10%.

First, the production matrix (S), intermediate consumption matrix (C), and final demand matrix (Y) from the SUTs are defined. Then, matrices C and Y are used to build the use matrix (U).

$$
S = \begin{bmatrix} 5,900 & 30 & 0 \\ 100 & 15,000 & 70 \\ 150 & 560 & 55,410 \end{bmatrix}, \quad
C = \begin{bmatrix} 1000 & 2500 & 410 \\ 1400 & 5000 & 8,900 \\ 500 & 1790 & 15,070 \end{bmatrix},
$$

$$
Y = \begin{bmatrix} 2,200 & 0 & 0 & 640 & 1,695 \\ 20,000 & 0 & 0 & 2,800 & 7,058 \\ 13,080 & 240 & 6,480 & 7,840 & 9,577 \end{bmatrix}
$$

		AGR	MFG	SER	HH	NPISH	Gov	GFCF	CII	X
	AGR	1,000	2,500	410	2,200	0	0	640	85	1,695
$U =$	MFG	1,400	5,000	8,900	20,000	0	0	2,800	70	7,058
	SER	500	1,790	15,070	13,080	240	6,480	7,840	0	9,577

Based on assumptions about the economy and tax legislation, the policy matrices, which take the dimension of matrix U, are defined. The process begins with the nontax object matrix (ϕ). Based on assumption number 2, all the outputs of NPISH and government are nonmarket production. The proportion of U that is not a taxable object, and that is 100% of all NPISH and government final consumption, is then derived.

$$\phi = \begin{array}{c} \\ \text{AGR} \\ \\ \text{MFG} \\ \\ \text{SER} \end{array} \begin{bmatrix} \begin{array}{ccccccccc} \text{AGR} & \text{MFG} & \text{SER} & \text{HH} & \text{NPISH} & \text{Gov} & \text{GFCF} & \text{CII} & \text{X} \\ 0 & 0 & 0 & 0 & 1 & 1 & 0 & 0 & 0 \\ 0 & 0 & 0 & 0 & 1 & 1 & 0 & 0 & 0 \\ 0 & 0 & 0 & 0 & 1 & 1 & 0 & 0 & 0 \end{array} \end{bmatrix}$$

Next, the VAT-exempt matrix (**E**) is populated. Based on assumption number 1, 100% of agricultural products are VAT-exempt.

$$\mathbf{E} = \begin{array}{c} \\ \text{AGR} \\ \\ \text{MFG} \\ \\ \text{SER} \end{array} \begin{bmatrix} \begin{array}{ccccccccc} \text{AGR} & \text{MFG} & \text{SER} & \text{HH} & \text{NPISH} & \text{Gov} & \text{GFCF} & \text{CII} & \text{X} \\ 1 & 1 & 1 & 1 & 1 & 1 & 1 & 1 & 1 \\ 0 & 0 & 0 & 0 & 0 & 0 & 0 & 0 & 0 \\ 0 & 0 & 0 & 0 & 0 & 0 & 0 & 0 & 0 \end{array} \end{bmatrix}$$

Based on assumption number 4, all exports are zero-rated. This populates the zero-rated matrix (**Z**).

$$\mathbf{Z} = \begin{array}{c} \\ \text{AGR} \\ \\ \text{MFG} \\ \\ \text{SER} \end{array} \begin{bmatrix} \begin{array}{ccccccccc} \text{AGR} & \text{MFG} & \text{SER} & \text{HH} & \text{NPISH} & \text{Gov} & \text{GFCF} & \text{CII} & \text{X} \\ 0 & 0 & 0 & 0 & 0 & 0 & 0 & 0 & 1 \\ 0 & 0 & 0 & 0 & 0 & 0 & 0 & 0 & 1 \\ 0 & 0 & 0 & 0 & 0 & 0 & 0 & 0 & 1 \end{array} \end{bmatrix}$$

Defining the input tax credit matrix involves several steps. First, the exempt supply matrix $\mathbf{S} \times \mathbf{E_C}$ is derived; where is $\mathbf{E_C}$ a subset of matrix $\mathbf{E}$ pertaining to the 3 × 3 submatrix related to intermediate consumption.

$$\mathbf{E_C} = \begin{array}{c} \\ \text{AGR} \\ \\ \text{MFG} \\ \\ \text{SER} \end{array} \begin{bmatrix} \begin{array}{ccc} \text{AGR} & \text{MFG} & \text{SER} \\ 1 & 1 & 1 \\ 0 & 0 & 0 \\ 0 & 0 & 0 \end{array} \end{bmatrix}$$

Based on assumption number 3, nonmarket output of NPISH and government is 20% of services. This means that 20% of services are not sold in the market. Therefore, the related input tax credits cannot be claimed (no output VAT to remit). Thus, matrices $\mathbf{E_C}$ to $\mathbf{E_C}^*$ are modified to reflect this.

$$\mathbf{E_C}^* = \begin{array}{c} \\ \text{AGR} \\ \text{MFG} \\ \text{SER} \end{array} \begin{array}{ccc} \text{AGR} & \text{MFG} & \text{SER} \\ \begin{bmatrix} 1 & 1 & 1 \\ 0 & 0 & 0 \\ 0 & 0 & 0.20 \end{bmatrix} \end{array}$$

The exempt supply matrix is $\mathbf{S} \times \mathbf{E_C}^*$ reflects the output that cannot claim input tax credits.

$$\mathbf{S} \times \mathbf{E_C}^* = \begin{array}{c} \\ \text{AGR} \\ \text{MFG} \\ \text{SER} \end{array} \begin{array}{ccc} \text{AGR} & \text{MFG} & \text{SER} \\ \begin{bmatrix} 5,900 & 30 & 0 \\ 0 & 0 & 0 \\ 0 & 0 & 11,082 \end{bmatrix} \end{array}$$

Then, the total supply that cannot claim input tax credits $\mathbf{i}'\,(\mathbf{S} \times \mathbf{E_C}^*)$ is define. This is simply the column sum of the exempt supply matrix which is used to estimate the proportion of total supply that cannot claim input tax credits .

$$\mathbf{i}'\,(\mathbf{S} \times \mathbf{E_C}^*) = \begin{array}{ccc} \text{AGR} & \text{MFG} & \text{SER} \\ \begin{bmatrix} 5,900 & 30 & 11,082 \end{bmatrix} \end{array}$$

$$\frac{\mathbf{i}'(\mathbf{S} \times \mathbf{E_C})}{\mathbf{i}'\mathbf{S}} = \begin{array}{ccc} \text{AGR} & \text{MFG} & \text{SER} \\ \begin{bmatrix} 0.9593 & 0.0019 & 0.1997 \end{bmatrix} \end{array}$$

is the proportion of total supply that cannot claim input tax credits. Here 95.93% of agriculture cannot claim input tax credits despite agricultural products being fully VAT-exempt. This is because agriculture also sells secondary products in VAT-taxable manufacturing and service sectors. Likewise, a small portion of manufacturing (0.19%) cannot claim input tax credits because of their secondary agricultural products.

The converse of the proportion of total supply that cannot claim input tax credits is the proportion that can claim input tax credits. It is computed using $\mathbf{h}' = \mathbf{i}' - \frac{\mathbf{i}'\,(\mathbf{S} \times \mathbf{E_C})}{\mathbf{i}'\,\mathbf{S}}$.

$$\mathbf{h}' = \begin{array}{ccc} \text{AGR} & \text{MFG} & \text{SER} \\ \begin{bmatrix} 0.0407 & 0.9981 & 0.8003 \end{bmatrix} \end{array}$$

The input tax credit $\mathbf{H}$ matrix is compiled by populating the submatrix related to intermediate consumption $\mathbf{H}_C = \mathbf{i}_m \otimes \mathbf{h}'$. The submatrix related to final demand $\mathbf{H}_Y$ is populated with zeroes because final consumers cannot claim input tax credits except for gross fixed capital formation. Based on assumption 5, all capital formation is undertaken by firms that can claim input tax credits. Therefore, 100% of GFCF is eligible for input tax credits.

	AGR	MFG	SER	HH	NPISH	Gov	GFCF	CII	X
AGR	0.0407	0.9981	0.8003	0	0	0	1	0	0
$\mathbf{H}_Y =$ MFG	0.0407	0.9981	0.8003	0	0	0	1	0	0
SER	0.0407	0.9981	0.8003	0	0	0	1	0	0

The preceding steps result in policy matrices $\boldsymbol{\phi}$, $\mathbf{E}$, $\mathbf{Z}$, and $\mathbf{H}$ required to define the taxable proportion. The taxable proportion of product i used by user j is given by $\pi_{ij} = (1 - \phi_{ij}) \cdot (1 - \epsilon_{ij}) \cdot (1 - \zeta_{ij}) \cdot (1 - \iota_{ij})$, where ϕ_{ij}, ϵ_{ij}, ζ_{ij}, and ι_{ij} are the respective proportions of product i used by user j that is a nontax object, VAT-exempt, zero-rated, and can be claimed as input tax credits. The next steps are to compute the taxable proportion of each product i used by user j, and then aggregate π_{ij} to Π.

	AGR	MFG	SER	HH	NPISH	Gov	GFCF	CII	X
AGR	0	0	0	0	0	0	0	0	0
$\Pi =$ MFG	0.9593	0.0019	0.1997	1	0	0	0	0	0
SER	0.9593	0.0019	0.1997	1	0	0	0	0	0

Based on fact number 6, the standard rate of VAT (τ) is 10%. Given the taxable proportions of each product i used by user j, the nonrecoverable $r_{ij} = \frac{\tau \pi_{ij}}{1 + \tau \pi_{ij}}$ rate is computed, which then is aggregated to give $\mathbf{R}$.

	AGR	MFG	SER	HH	NPISH	Gov	GFCF	CII	X
AGR	0	0	0	0	0	0	0	0	0
$\mathbf{R} =$ MFG	0.0875	0.0002	0.0196	0.0909	0	0	0	0	0
SER	0.0875	0.0002	0.0196	0.0909	0	0	0	0	0

Finally, the theoretical VAT attributable to the economy is given by $\mathbf{T} = \mathbf{U} \times \mathbf{R}$.

$$\mathbf{T} = \begin{array}{c} \text{AGR} \\ \text{MFG} \\ \text{SER} \end{array} \begin{array}{ccccccccc} \text{AGR} & \text{MFG} & \text{SER} & \text{HH} & \text{NPISH} & \text{Gov} & \text{GFCF} & \text{CII} & \text{X} \\ 0 & 0 & 0 & 0 & 0 & 0 & 0 & 0 & 0 \\ 123 & 1 & 174 & 1{,}818 & 0 & 0 & 0 & 0 & 0 \\ 44 & 0 & 295 & 1{,}189 & 0 & 0 & 0 & 0 & 0 \end{array}$$

Summing across the matrix , the total theoretical VAT is **$3,644**. When the theoretical estimate is compared with the actual VAT of **$3,545**, the **VAT gap** is **$99** resulting in a **theoretical VAT ratio (TVR)** of **97%**. To derive the actual VAT valuation matrix as well as the VAT that factors in the supply table, the TVR is multiplied by matrix **T**.

$$\mathbf{T}_{actual} = \begin{array}{c} \text{AGR} \\ \text{MFG} \\ \text{SER} \end{array} \begin{array}{ccccccccc} \text{AGR} & \text{MFG} & \text{SER} & \text{HH} & \text{NPISH} & \text{Gov} & \text{GFCF} & \text{CII} & \text{X} \\ 0 & 0 & 0 & 0 & 0 & 0 & 0 & 0 & 0 \\ 119 & 1 & 170 & 1{,}769 & 0 & 0 & 0 & 0 & 0 \\ 43 & 0 & 287 & 1{,}157 & 0 & 0 & 0 & 0 & 0 \end{array}$$

To obtain the vector of VAT on products that will form part of the supply table, sum each row of the actual VAT valuation matrix.[1]

Actual VAT Valuation Matrix

Item	AGR Sector	MFG Sector	SER Sector	Total VAT Borne by Producer	VAT on Final Consumption HH	NPISH	Gov	GFCF	CII	X	VAT on Products
AGR product	–	–	–	–	–	–	–	–	–	–	–
MFG product	119	1	170	**290**	1,769	–	–	–	–	–	**2,058**
SER product	43	0	287	**330**	1,157	–	–	–	–	–	**1,487**
Subtotal	**162**	**1**	**457**	**620**	**2,925**	**–**	**–**	**–**	**–**	**–**	**3,545**
GVA	–	–	–	–							
VAT by sector	**128**	**1**	**361**	**620**							

AGR = agriculture; CII = changes in inventory; GFCF = gross fixed capital formation; Gov = government; GVA = gross value-added; HH = households; MFG = manufacturing; NPISH = nonprofit institution serving households; SER = services; VAT = value-added tax; X = exports.
Source: Authors.

[1] Note that if the incorporation of the vector of VAT on products in the supply table renders it imbalanced with the use table, then rebalancing is made by the national accountant using knowledgeable assessments. The NAS-VAT model is employed in an iterative process until the discrepancy between the supply and use tables is nil.

VALUE-ADDED TAX REGIME FOR ARMENIA, KAZAKHSTAN, AND UZBEKISTAN

The value- added tax (VAT) regime is described by the policy variables and the standard rate of VAT. When aggregated, the respective policy variables ϕ_{ij}, ϵ_{ij}, ζ_{ij}, and ι_{ij} will define the policy matrices $\boldsymbol{\phi}$, $\mathbf{E}$, $\mathbf{Z}$, and $\mathbf{H}$. The contents of the VAT-Exempt Matrix $\mathbf{E}$ and the Input Tax Credit Matrix $\mathbf{H}$ are jointly determined using data on VAT-exempt products and non-VAT-registered businesses (typically micro and small enterprises) that also sell VAT-exempt products and cannot claim input tax credits.[1]

2.1.1. Armenia

The standard rate of VAT in Armenia is 20% for 2017 and 2018. Table A2.1.1 indicates the VAT-exempt products in Armenia, which will define its policy matrix . A number of these products, namely health care, education, and financial services are VAT-exempt following the broad consensus on products to exempt from VAT. The others are considered nonstandard in the existing VAT literature (Ebrill et al. 2001). In addition to the products in Table A2.1.1, goods and services sold by businesses with annual turnover not exceeding AMD 58.35 million (approximately US$120,000) that did not register as VAT payers are VAT-exempt.[2]

Table A2.1.1: VAT-Exempt Products in Armenia

Health care	Agricultural machinery
Education	Animal and vegetable fertilizers
Passenger transportation	Pesticides and disinfectants
Utilities	Coconuts
Social services	Vegetable textile fibers
Financial services	Cotton seeds
Gambling services	Flower seeds and other seeds
Educational books	Carpets and rugs
Research and development activities	Newspapers
Pharmaceutical products	Precious stones and metals
Funeral services	Unmanufactured tobacco
Services by religious organizations	Insurance services
Legal and licensing services	

VAT = value-added tax.
Source: Tax Code of the Republic of Armenia (adopted on 4 October 2016).

---

[1] In the absence of disaggregated data on non-VAT registration, it is assumed that most formal businesses, if given the chance, will opt to register for VAT to take advantage of the input-credit mechanism. Therefore, it is assumed that only the non-observed economy is not registered with internal revenue authorities.

[2] AMD 58.35 million is approximately $120,878.53 at a then prevailing exchange rate of AMD 482.716/$1 (International Monetary Fund 2021). Businesses with annual turnover not exceeding this level may opt to register as VAT payers. If so, their sales have output VAT, and they could correspondingly claim the related input VAT on purchases.

For zero-rated products, Armenia follows the destination principle and zero-rated exports, international transport and cargo, and the fuel consumed related to international transport and cargo. Data from this populates the zero-rated matrix .

2.1.2. Kazakhstan

The standard rate of VAT in Kazakhstan is 12% for 2017 to 2019. Table A2.1.2 indicates the VAT-exempt products in Kazakhstan, which will define its policy matrix . Similar to Armenia, health care, education, and financial services are VAT-exempt. Compared to the VAT regime of Armenia, there are fewer nonstandard VAT-exempt products. The VAT regime of Kazakhstan is more broadly based compared with Armenia.[3]

Table A2.1.2: VAT-Exempt Products in Kazakhstan

Land and residential buildings Services by noncommercial organizations Services in the areas of culture, science, and education	Financial services Goods and services related to medical and veterinary activities Goods imported by individuals not for entrepreneurial purposes

VAT = value-added tax.
Source: Code of the Republic of Kazakhstan dated 10 December 2008 No. 99-IV, 25 December 2017 No. 120-VI.

Kazakhstan also adopts the destination principle. Exports, international transport and cargo, and the fuel consumed related to international transport and cargo are zero-rated. Additionally, Kazakhstan determines the sale of fine gold and sales of goods to Special Economic Zones to be zero-rated.

In 2018, Kazakhstan implemented a reform to its VAT legislation.[4] Amendments were made particularly on VAT administration, with the setting up of the VAT control account. On taxability of certain products, the reform clarified that input VAT related to construction in progress can be claimed against output VAT. Moreover, the sale and lease of residential buildings are already subject to VAT (no longer VAT-exempt).

---

[3] A broader-based VAT regime affords the jurisdiction a lower standard rate of VAT. Because the VAT regime of Kazakhstan has a broader base, it can afford a lower standard rate of 12%. Armenia, which has more VAT-exempt products, has a higher standard rate of VAT of 20%.

[4] The Law on Taxes and Other Obligatory State Budget Payments was enacted on 25 December 2017 in Kazakhstan.

2.1.3. Uzbekistan

The standard rate of VAT in Uzbekistan was 20% from 2016 to 2018. Following tax reform in 2019, in the third quarter of 2019, the standard rate of VAT was reduced to 15%. Table A2.1.3 indicates the VAT-exempt products in Uzbekistan, which will define its policy matrix . Beginning in 2019, a VAT registration revenue threshold was introduced whereby entities with revenue exceeding UZS 1 billion (approximately US$113,000) are mandated to register as VAT payers. Business entities not registered as VAT payers are not required to remit output VAT. Hence, their output is VAT-exempt.

Table A2.1.3: VAT-Exempt Products in Uzbekistan

Public administration	Medical and dental instruments
Education	Passenger transport
Residential care services for older people and people with disabilities	Health services
	Veterinary services
Services by religious organizations	Financial services
Funeral and related services	Insurance services
Basic pharmaceutical products	

VAT = value-added tax.
Source: Tax Code of the Republic of Uzbekistan (adopted on 1 January 2008).

To characterize the policy matrix , goods and services that are zero-rated are identified. Unlike in Armenia and Kazakhstan, some goods and services other than those exported are also zero-rated. These include precious metals, electricity, gas, and water services.

THEORETICAL VAT BY USE CATEGORIES

The nonrecoverable value-added tax (VAT) on products is estimated for Armenia in 2017 to 2018, Kazakhstan from 2017 to 2019, and Uzbekistan from 2016 to 2019. Table A2.2 summarizes the theoretical VAT by three use categories–intermediate consumption (IC), household final consumption, and gross fixed capital formation (GFCF)–in millions of local currencies.[1]

Table A2.2: Theoretical Value-Added Tax on Products by Use Categories

In millions of local currencies

Nonrecoverable VAT on:	Armenia		Kazakhstan			Uzbekistan			
	2017	2018	2017	2018	2019	2016	2017	2018	2019
Intermediate consumption	121,696	132,470	712,210	992,435	981,470	6,727,784	7,734,750	11,051,326	15,041,095
Household consumption	342,937	360,749	1,736,084	1,875,102	2,125,538	12,615,478	15,036,723	20,431,196	25,253,447
Gross fixed capital formation	63,986	54,471	159,878	197,754	192,447	982,683	1,297,175	2,431,919	3,079,987
Total theoretical VAT	**528,620**	**547,689**	**2,608,172**	**3,065,291**	**3,299,455**	**20,325,945**	**24,068,648**	**33,914,442**	**43,374,529**

VAT = value-added tax.
Note: Local currency in Armenia is AMD, Kazakhstan is KZT, and Uzbekistan is UZS.
Source: Estimates using the NAS-VAT model.

Figure A2.3 shows the structure of nonrecoverable VAT estimates by the three use categories. As expected, VAT in household consumption in Armenia, Kazakhstan, and Uzbekistan comprise the largest share in nonrecoverable VAT, ranging from 58% to 66% from 2017 to 2019. Meanwhile, VAT-exempt producers in the same economies absorb approximately 24 to 34% of total nonrecoverable VAT over the same period (nonrecoverable VAT on IC).

---

[1] By virtue of the nonmarket nature of general government final consumption and nonprofit institutions serving households (NPISH) final consumption, no VAT is calculated on the final demand side. Only the related nonrecoverable input VAT in the production-side affects the VAT estimate.

Figure A2.3: Structure of Nonrecoverable VAT by Use Categories

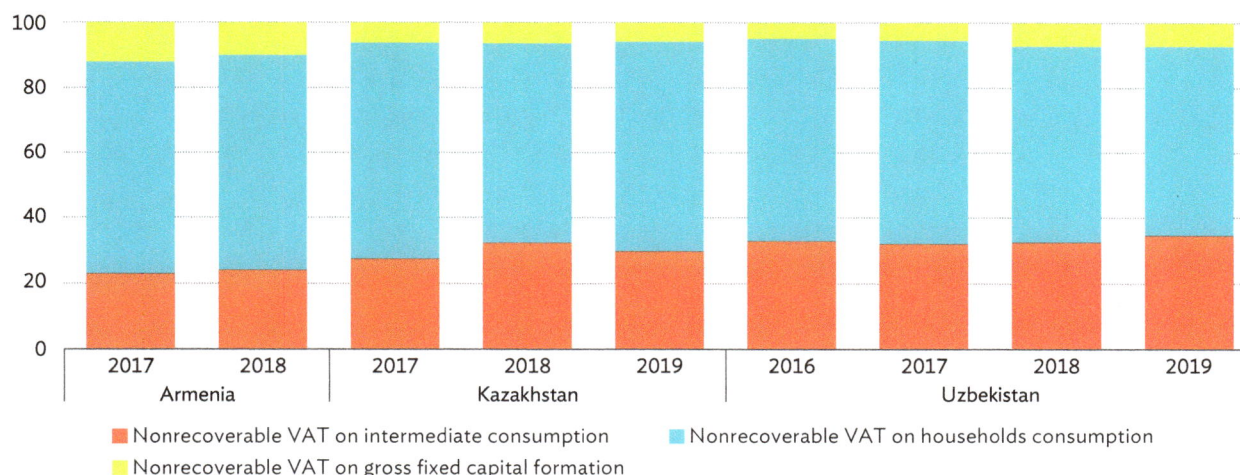

VAT = value-added tax.
Source: Estimates using the NAS-VAT model.

The share in nonrecoverable VAT is the lowest for GFCF. It ranges from 5% to 12% from 2017 to 2019 in Armenia, Kazakhstan, and Uzbekistan. GFCF usually requires large capital outlay, and thus, it is unlikely for micro and small enterprises falling below the revenue threshold and for informal enterprises to invest in large amounts of GFCF. Therefore, VAT on GFCF is commonly only nonrecoverable for formal enterprises that sell VAT-exempt products like schools, hospitals, and banks. Most VAT on GFCF is recoverable by large VAT-registered formal enterprises.

Total theoretical VAT of the three economies is observed to be increasing through time. This is mainly because of the increasing use (in nominal terms) of output across the years. This trend is observed in Armenia as VAT on intermediate consumption and household final consumption expenditure increased between 2017 and 2018. A lower VAT for GFCF was estimated from 2017 to 2018. A longer series will be needed to draw conclusions from this observation, as capital investments by enterprises are highly volatile thus the analysis might be narrow on this specific component.

For Uzbekistan, the trend of increasing VAT over time holds true as the consumption and investment of VAT-exempt producers and households had been increasing from 2016 to 2019. The increase in theoretical VAT between 2018 and 2019 likewise indicates that the increase in nominal consumption was high enough to offset the potential decline in theoretical VAT due to the reduction of the standard rate from 20% to 15% in the fourth quarter of 2019.

In Kazakhstan, VAT on household consumption had been increasing from 2017 to 2019. Meanwhile, VAT on IC and GFCF increased between 2017 and 2018 but marginally declined between 2018 and 2019. Various systemic changes occurred in Kazakhstan beginning in 2018, including the introduction of VAT reform (i.e., taxability of the sale and lease of residential buildings) and the gradual decline in the output of illegal activity.[2] Both changes are expected to broaden the VAT base and, holding the relative consumption of VAT-exempt producers constant, increase theoretical VAT on household consumption while decreasing VAT absorbed in IC beginning in 2018. However, the changes in consumption patterns of VAT-exempt producers overall resulted in an increase in nonrecoverable VAT on IC and GFCF in 2018.

[2]   In Kazakhstan, the share of output of illegal activity from total output was 28.7% in 2017, followed by 27.2% in 2018 and 23.7% in 2019.

DATA SOURCES FOR VAT ESTIMATIONS FOR ARMENIA, KAZAKHSTAN, AND UZBEKISTAN

Source	Armenia	Kazakhstan	Uzbekistan
Primary data source	Experimental Supply and Use Tables 2017-2018	Experimental Supply and Use Tables 2017-2019	Experimental Supply and Use Tables 2016-2019
	State Budget Revenue Report 2017-2018	State Budget Execution Report 2017-2019	State Budget Execution Report 2016–2019
	Tax Code of the Republic of Armenia (adopted on 4 October 2016)	Code of the Republic of Kazakhstan dated 10 December 2008 No. 99-IV Code of the Republic of Kazakhstan of 25 December 2017 No. 120-VI	Tax Code of the Republic of Uzbekistan (adopted on 1 January 2008)
Secondary data sources			
Purpose			
1. **Estimation of non-VAT-registered taxpayers and non-registered (informal) businesses**	• Value Added By the Size of Enterprise Engaged in Entrepreneurial Activity Determined By Number of Employees in 2016 (ARMStat) • Count of VAT payers and registered non-VAT payers (State Revenue Committee of Armenia)	• 2017–2019 supply and use table by institutional sector (KAZ BNS)	• Publication on small business of Uzbekistan (UZB SSC) • Estimates of non-observed economy (UZB SSC)
2. **Estimation of the gross fixed capital formation matrix**	• Gross fixed capital formation by types of economic activity (ARMStat) • Main Indicators of Construction (ARMStat) • Exports and Imports of the Republic of Armenia by indicators, foreign trade and years 2016–2018 (ARMStat)	• Fixed assets of Kazakhstan (KAZ BNS) • Investment and construction activities in the Republic of Kazakhstan (KAZ BNS)	• Fixed assets of Uzbekistan (UZB SSC) • Investments in Fixed Assets by types of economic activity (UZB SSC) • Imports trade data (UZB SSC)
3. **Estimation of ownership of dwellings**	• Ownership of dwellings available in the SUTs (ARMStat)	• Owner occupied dwellings calculations for National accounts compilation (KAZ BNS)	• Owner occupied dwellings calculations for National accounts compilation (UZB SSC)

VALUE-ADDED TAX IN ADB DEVELOPING MEMBER COUNTRIES

ADB Developing Member Countries	Adoption of VAT	Standard Rate[a]	Revenue Threshold in LC[b]	Revenue Threshold in USD[b]
Armenia	1993	20%	AMD115 million	228,279
Azerbaijan	1992	18%	AZN200,000	117,647
Bangladesh	1991	15%	BDT8 million	94,025
Bhutan	Deferred to 2024	7%	BTN5 million	67,623
Cambodia	1997	10%	KHR125 million (sales of goods for the past three months) KHR60 millions (sales of services for the past three months)	30,497 (sales of goods for the past three months) 14,639 (sales of services for the past three months)
People's Republic of China	1984	13%	RMB5 million	775,317
Cook Islands	1997	15%	NZD40,000	28,293
Fiji	1992	15% supply of goods 9% supply of services	FJD300,000	144,883
Georgia	1994	18%	GEL100,000	31,041
India	2005 (General Sales Tax was introduced in 2017, with features similar to VAT)	Various rates of general sales tax	INR2 million	27,057
Indonesia	1985	11% (2022) 12% (2025)	IDR4.8 billion	97,846
Kazakhstan	1990	12%	KZT61.26 million	143,834
Kiribati	2014	12.5%	AUD100,000	75,119
Kyrgyz Republic	1996	12%	KGS30 million	354,439
Lao People's Democratic Republic	2010	7%	–	–
Malaysia	2015-2018	–	–	–
Maldives	2011	6%- supply of goods and services 12%- supply of tourism goods and services	–	–

continued on next page

Appendix 4 *continued*

ADB Developing Member Countries	Adoption of VAT	Standard Rate[a]	Revenue Threshold in LC[b]	Revenue Threshold in USD[b]
Marshall Islands				
Federated States of Micronesia				
Mongolia	2006	10%	MNT50 million	17,544
Nauru	–	–	–	–
Nepal	1997	13%	RS2 million	16,930
Pakistan	1990–1991	17%	PKR10 million	61,385
Palau	–	–	–	–
Papua New Guinea	1990s	10%	PGK250,000	71,250
Philippines	1998	12%	PHP3 million	60,908
Samoa	2015	15%	$130,000	50,859
Solomon Islands				
Sri Lanka	2002	8%	LKR300 million	
Tajikistan	2013	Standard rate – 18% Reduced rate – 5% for taxable supplies (except imports) made by catering, wholesale, and retail trade companies, sales and supply agencies, educational institutions, and construction firms.	TJS500,000	44,213
Thailand	1992	7%	THB1.8 million	56,290
Timor-Leste	–	–	–	–
Tonga	2003	15%	$100,000	44,151
Turkmenistan	2004	15%	–	–
Tuvalu	2008	Determined by the Minster of Regulation; between 3% and 10%	$100,00	75,119
Uzbekistan	1992	15%	UZS1 billion	94,255
Vanuatu	1998	12.5%	VT4 million	36,546
Viet Nam	1999	10%	–	–

ADB = Asian Development Bank, LC = local currency, USD = United States dollar, VAT = value-added tax.
Notes:
[a] As of August 2022.
[b] Using LC: USD exchange rate from the International Monetary Fund (IMF) International Financial Statistics (IFS) in 2021, accessed on 17 August 2022. For economies with exchange rates not in the IMF IFS Database (Fiji, Georgia, India, Indonesia, ...), the official exchange rate period average is from the World Bank World Development Indicators, accessed on 29 August 2022.
Sources:
Pricewaterhouse Coopers (PwC) Worldwide Tax Summaries 2022. https://taxsummaries.pwc.com.
National Board of Revenue, Bangladesh. https://nbr.gov.bd/faq/vat-faq/eng.
Ministry of Finance, Royal Government of Bhutan. https://www.mof.gov.bt/wp-content/uploads/2020/07/NotificationGST.pdf.
Ministry of Economy and Finance, General Department of Taxation, Kingdom of Cambodia. https://aseanvaluer.org/images/PDF/The%20 Tax%20System%20of%20the%20Kingdom%20of%20Cambodia.pdf.

continued on next page

Appendix 4 *continued*

Dezan Shira & Associates. https://www.china-briefing.com/news/chinas-tax-incentives-for-small-businesses/.
Ministry of Finance & Economic Management, Government of the Cook Islands. http://www.mfem.gov.ck/rmd-tax/rmd-tax-types/rmd-value-added-tax.
BDO Global. https://www.bdo.global/en-gb/microsites/tax-newsletters/indirect-tax-news/issue-1-2022/indonesia-vat-rate-increase-and-other-changes-to-vat-rules.
Orbitax Tax Hub. https://www.orbitax.com/news/archive.php/Kazakhstan-Confirms-Reduced-VA-49212/.
OECD Consumption Tax Trends 2020. https://www.oecd-ilibrary.org/sites/1ca62ced-en/index.html?itemId=/content/component/1ca62ced-en.
KYRGYZ REPUBLIC- https://www.libertas-institut.com/de/Mittel-Osteuropa/Tax%20Code.pdf.
LAO PDR- https://documents.worldbank.org/en/publication/documents-reports/documentdetail/494641468046131867/rolling-out-value-added-tax-in-lao-pdr-issues-for-effective-implementation.
MALAYSIA- https://core.ac.uk/download/pdf/82527915.pdf; https://www.ey.com/en_gl/tax/how-vat-took-over-the-tax-world.
MALDIVES- https://vatcalculatorg.com/vat-calculator-maldives/.
MARSHALL ISLANDS- https://gsl.org/en/taxes/tax-zones/marshall-islands/.
MONGOLIA- https://policy.asiapacificenergy.org/sites/default/files/Law%20on%20Value%20Added%20Tax%20of%202006%20%28EN%29.pdf.
NEPAL- https://nepal.gov.np:8443/NationalPortal/view-page?id=94.
PAKISTAN- https://www.vatcalc.com/pakistan/pakistan-cuts-sales-tax-threshold/; https://core.ac.uk/download/pdf/234647134.pdf.
PAPUA NEW GUINEA- https://taxsummaries.pwc.com/papua-new-guinea/corporate/other-taxes; https://pngnri.org/images/Publications/DP142_-_201410_-_Odhuno_-_Taxation_Policies.pdf.
SAMOA - https://www.revenue.gov.ws/wp-content/uploads/2020/10/Value-Added-Goods-and-Services-Tax-Act-2015.pdf
TAJIKISTAN - https://tpp.tj/put2011/pdf/rules/en/1.pdf.
TONGA - https://www.revenue.gov.to/sites/default/files/inline-files/ConsumptionTaxAct2003.pdf
International Tax Turkmenistan Highlights Castro and Co. International - https://www.castroandco.com/documents/Castro-Co.-Turkmenistan-Highlights.pdf.
TUVALU - https://tuvalu.tradeportal.org/media/ConsumptionTaxAct2008_1.pdf.
VANUATU - https://www.wto.org/english/thewto_e/acc_e/vut_e/wtaccvut8_leg_4.pdf.

REFERENCES

Ebrill, Liam, Michael Keen, Jean-Paul Bodin, and Victoria Summers. 2001. *The Modern VAT.* Washington D.C.: International Monetary Fund.

Ehrbar, Al. n.d. "Government Policy, Macroeconomics, Taxes: Consumption Tax." *The Library of Economics and Liberty.* Accessed August 21, 2022. https://www.econlib.org/library/Enc/ConsumptionTax.html.

European Commission. 2008. *Manual of Supply, Use and Input-Output Tables.* Luxembourg: Office for Official Publications of the European Communities.

Hutton, Eric. 2017. *The Revenue Administration—Gap Analysis Program: Model and Methodology for Value-Added Tax Gap Estimation.* Technical Notes and Manuals, Washington D.C.: International Monetary Fund.

HM Revenue and Customs. 2022. "Measuring tax gaps 2022 edition: tax gap estimates for 2020 to 2021." *GOV.UK.* June 3. https://www.gov.uk/government/statistics/measuring-tax-gaps.

James, Kathryn. 2015. *The Rise of the Value-Added Tax.* Cambridge: Cambridge University Press.

Kristoffersson, Eleonor. 2021. "Why do not all countries introduce a VAT/GST?" *Kluwer International Tax Blog.* March 3. https://kluwertaxblog.com/2021/03/03/why-do-not-all-countries-introduce-a-vat-gst/.

Medina, Leando, and Freidrich Schneider. 2018. *Shadow Economies Around the World: What Did We Learn Over the Last 20 Years?* Working Paper, Washington D.C.: International Monetary Fund.

Muthitacharoen, Athiphat, Wonma Wanichthaworn, and Trongwut Burong. 2021. "VAT threshold and small business behavior: evidence from Thai tax returns." *International Tax and Public Finance* (28): 1242-1275.

OECD. 2020. "Consumption Tax Trends 2020: VAT/GST and Excise Rates, Trends and Policy Issues." Paris: OECD Publishing.

Organisation for Economic Co-operation and Development. 2002. *Measuring the Non-Observed Economy.* Paris: OECD Publications Service.

Schnek, Alan, Victor Thuronyi, and Wei Cui. 2015. *Value Added Tax: A Comparative Approach.* Cambridge: Cambridge University Press.

ten Raa, Thijs. 2005. The Economics of Input-Output Analysis. Cambridge: Cambridge University Press.

United Nations. 2010. *System of National Accounts 2008.* New York: United Nations.

United Nations Economic Commission for Europe. 2008. *Non-Observed Economy In National Accounts: Survey of Country Practices.* New York and Geneva: United Nations Publication.

www.ingramcontent.com/pod-product-compliance
Lightning Source LLC
Chambersburg PA
CBHW042034220326
41599CB00045BA/7391